'This resource provides strategies for supporting the communication and daily of young and older children with autism. The authors have translated current research into naturalistic interventions and contemporary practices into simple and clear stra ensuring their practical application in everyday contexts. I recommend this bo clinicians, teachers and anyone who supports children with autism and others experiencing communication difficulties.'

— *Teresa Iacono, PhD, Professor of Rural and Regional Allied Health, Faculty of Health Sciences, La Trobe University, Australia*

'This book provides a very valuable resource of step-by step visual instructions – picture scripts – for a range of everyday activities. Without being prescriptive in putting forward a particular "approach", the accompanying text in each chapter clearly explains the importance of using the visual strengths of children with autism and making their lives more predictable and easier to understand. Many of the scripts will be directly useful to teachers, parents and others involved with children with autism, and other communication difficulties, across a wide range of ages and abilities. The principles will enable many more personalized scripts to be developed to suit the individual child and his or her situation.'

— *Phil Christie, Consultant Child Psychologist, The Elizabeth Newson Centre*

'This comprehensive "how-to" book leaves no stone unturned! From the detailed instructions for caregivers to the carefully-rendered picture scripts that teach a wide variety of skills, Teach Me With Pictures and its accompanying CD-ROM puts an engaging, easy-to-implement intervention package into the hands of parents and professionals.'

— *Diane Twachtman-Cullen, PhD, CCC-SLP, Editor-in-Chief of* Autism Spectrum Quarterly

'The use of visual schedules/scripts has been endorsed as an evidence-based strategy for individuals with autism in a number of recent research reviews. Now, this clever book offers a user-friendly collection of visual scripts that will support the development of communication, play and daily living skills while saving valuable preparation time! Beautifully illustrated and practical, this is a must-have for both parents and clinicians.'

— *Pat Mirenda, PhD, BCBA-D, Professor in Department of Educational and Counselling Psychology, and Special Education, The University of British Columbia, Canada*

'Whether a child has the gift of speech or not, pictures are a powerful way of unlocking meaningful communication. As a parent of a daughter with severe autism, I understand the incredible frustration of feeling powerless to help my child. Improving communication with a tool such as picture scripts gives the child greater independence and gives the parent the ability to interact with their child. Teach Me with Pictures is an invaluable resource for anyone living or working with a child with autism. I wish we had had it when our daughter was young.'

— *Arthur Fleischmann, father of Carly Fleischmann and co- author of* Carly's Voice: Breaking Through Autism

Teach Me *With* Pictures

by the same author

Motivate to Communicate!
300 Games and Activities for Your Child with Autism
Simone Griffin and Dianne Sandler
ISBN 978 1 84905 041 8
eISBN 978 0 85700 215 0

of related interest

Exploring Feelings for Young Children with High-Functioning Autism or Asperger's Disorder
The STAMP Treatment Manual
Angela Scarpa, Anthony Wells and Tony Attwood
ISBN 978 1 84905 920 6
eISBN 978 0 85700 681 3

Teaching Theory of Mind
A Curriculum for Children with High Functioning Autism,
Asperger's Syndrome, and Related Social Challenges
Kirstina Ordetx
Foreword by Susan J. Moreno
ISBN 978 1 84905 897 1

Speak, Move, Play and Learn with Children on the Autism Spectrum
Activities to Boost Communication Skills, Sensory Integration and Coordination Using
Simple Ideas from Speech and Language Pathology and Occupational Therapy
Lois Jean Brady, America X Gonzalez, Maciej Zawadzki and Corinda Presley
Illustrated by Byron Roy James
ISBN 978 1 84905 872 8
eISBN 978 0 85700 531 1

Social Communication Cues for Young Children with Autism
Spectrum Disorders and Related Conditions
How to Give Great Greetings, Pay Cool Compliments and Have Fun with Friends
Tarin Varughese
ISBN 978 1 84905 870 4
eISBN 978 0 85700 506 9

Teach Me
With Pictures

40 Fun Picture Scripts to Develop Play and Communication Skills in Children on the Autism Spectrum

Simone Griffin,
Ruth Harris and
Linda Hodgdon

Illustrated by Ralph Butler

Jessica Kingsley *Publishers*
London and Philadelphia

First published in 2013
by Jessica Kingsley Publishers
116 Pentonville Road
London N1 9JB, UK
and
400 Market Street, Suite 400
Philadelphia, PA 19106, USA

www.jkp.com

Library of Congress Cataloging in Publication Data
Griffin, Simone.
  Teach me with pictures : 40 fun picture scripts to develop play and communication skills in children on the autism spectrum / Simone Griffin, Ruth Harris and Linda Hodgdon ; illustrated by Ralph Butler.
      pages cm
  ISBN 978-1-84905-201-6 (alk. paper)
 1. Autistic children--Rehabilitation. 2. Interpersonal communication--Study and teaching. 3. Special education--Audio visual aids. 4. Play therapy. I. Harris, Ruth (Speech and language therapist) II. Hodgdon, Linda A. III. Title.
  RJ506.A9G755 2013
  618.92'891653--dc23
                                        2013012244

British Library Cataloguing in Publication Data
A CIP catalogue record for this book is available from the British Library

ISBN 978 1 84905 201 6
eISBN 978 0 85700 632 5

Printed and bound in Great Britain

CONTENTS

Chapter 1

INTRODUCTION

WHAT ARE PICTURE SCRIPTS?

Have you ever tried to assemble flat-pack furniture without reading the instructions? If so, you probably remember the frustration of struggling with what appeared to be a simple task. No doubt you quickly realized that it wasn't as easy as you first thought and that you had to complete several steps in the right order for all the pieces to fit together.

It is hoped that you were able to assemble your furniture by following the picture instructions step-by-step. If you were successful, then your coffee table or wardrobe will have matched the picture on the front of the box!

This is just how a picture script is used.

A picture script is a set of instructions that breaks down a complex task into smaller steps. Pictures and words are used to help explain each step. Step-by-step instructions presented this way can make learning new skills easier for everyone, but especially for children with autism, who are often visual learners.

ABOUT THIS BOOK

The book provides 40 sample picture scripts of activities designed for children with autism aged three to ten years old. Children with other communication, language or learning disabilities can also benefit from using picture scripts.

The picture scripts have been carefully chosen to reflect the play and classroom activities of typically developing children of this age group. A survey of teachers was conducted to identify typical classroom activities of six-year-old children. The results of that survey contributed to our activity choices. We believe it is important to teach activities to children with autism which can provide them with the skills necessary to participate in the same activities as their peers.

The scripts are organized into six chapters from the practical 'Everyday Living' life skills, such as 'Brush Your Teeth' and 'Set the Table', to the fun 'Cupcakes' (in the 'Cooking' chapter) or 'Picture Frame' (in 'Arts and Crafts'). The variety of sample scripts demonstrates how picture scripts can be used in many parts of a child's life.

The picture scripts are designed to be photocopied from the book or printed in colour from the CD-ROM which accompanies the book. Each page of this book contains three picture script 'steps' which are designed to be cut up and fixed together (e.g. stapled/keyrings) to make a small book (see page 10).

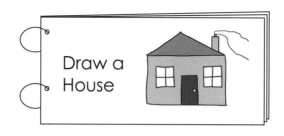

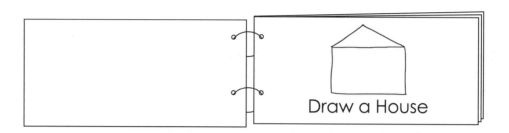

With the right support, the picture scripts in this book can be used to help teach children with autism new communication and play skills. Our main goal is to show you how picture scripts work and to provide some successful examples to get you started. You will then be able to develop your own scripts for your child or children in your life to help them learn other tasks and accomplish new goals.

PICTURE SCRIPTS AND AUTISM

We have used the term 'autism' throughout the book to refer to all children on the autism spectrum. Behaviours that characterize children with autism include:

- difficulties with social interaction and communication (verbal and non-verbal)
- repetitive behaviour and/or narrow, restricted interests.

In addition, it is common for children with autism to have:

- trouble with their 'executive function' (initiating, organizing themselves, planning ahead and maintaining attention)
- a tendency to focus on small details, struggling to work out the 'main event' in a situation
- 'sensory sensitivities', meaning that their experience of information received through the senses is often different – either 'too much' (e.g. noise or touch is unbearable) or 'not enough' (e.g. they need to move around constantly to feel physically stable).

The combination of these difficulties can make it challenging for children with autism to develop new play and life skills and to communicate and interact socially.

In contrast, most of these children tend to be *visual* learners. They frequently respond more positively to visual supports than to verbal directions. That is why using picture scripts enhances their engagement and motivation as we help them participate in play and learning activities.

FIVE REASONS WHY PICTURE SCRIPTS WORK

1. Pictures appeal to the *visual strengths* of children with autism.

2. Breaking down activities into *small steps* makes them achievable.

3. Picture scripts show the child exactly what to do. This gives confidence to children with autism by making the activities more *predictable*.

4. The language in the scripts is *simple and consistent*. Whoever carries out the activity with the child says the same words, making it easier for the child to understand.

5. Picture scripts act as a *memory aid*, increasing independence.

HOW DO PICTURE SCRIPTS BENEFIT CHILDREN WITH AUTISM?

Picture scripts are a versatile tool and can be used to help children with autism to develop new skills. Here are some examples.

Increased independence

Picture scripts can help children carry out steps of an activity that they previously relied on an adult to complete. They can move children on from being 'stuck', helping them learn a variety of actions or interactions in play.

Making choices

It is easy to offer children a choice of activity by showing them two or more picture scripts. This will keep them motivated! The 'Cooking' section includes choice boards, enabling children to choose their toppings by pointing or exchanging a picture.

Following instructions more easily

Picture scripts make it easier for children to understand by showing them small manageable steps through pictures and simple written language.

Extending play skills

Picture scripts open up opportunities for your child to learn new games by showing him how to play with toys.

More sociable play

Picture scripts make play activities more understandable and predictable for the child. This can make it easier for him to play around other children. Peers can join in and follow picture scripts and model activities for your child.

Copying actions

The actions in the picture script are the same each time. Children will learn more quickly when they can predict what is expected.

Remembering the steps of an activity

Picture scripts help children to complete an activity, instead of 'stalling' when they forget what comes next.

Playing in new places

Children with autism often have trouble 'generalizing' skills (doing the same activity in different places). The pictures in the scripts help them to see that it is the same game/activity, even though the setting is different.

Developing language skills

High motivation activities and use of simple language in the picture scripts create opportunities for your child to learn new vocabulary and to practise using it. See further ideas on page 19 ('Promoting language and communication skills').

HOW TO USE PICTURE SCRIPTS

Three crucial steps for success

Use these points to guide the activity you choose for your child:

1. *Motivation* – it needs to be fun! Choose activities which you believe will create a positive experience for your child.

2. *Skill level* – the activity needs to be easy enough for your child to achieve success.

3. *Your help* – you can make picture scripts a success for your child by giving the right amount of help at first and then reducing your involvement to help him towards independence.

1. Motivation, motivation, motivation!

It's easy for us to get excited about using a new approach to support our children, but if the activity itself is no fun for them, then they won't be interested in using the picture script. So remember, the picture script is only as good as the child's interest in the activity.

You do not need to use the activities in this book in any particular sequence. You'll have the best success when you start with a category of activities that your child demonstrates the most interest in. Once your child achieves some positive results, you can move on to other activities in other categories. Where do you think you will begin?

- Pretend Play
- Drawing Pictures
- Building and Construction Games
- Cooking
- Arts and Crafts
- Everyday Living.

Think about the things your child *already likes to play or do*, but needs help to:

- do more *frequently*
- complete more *independently*
- carry out more *socially*
- achieve in a *new setting*.

2. Your child's skill level

In order to increase the chance of success for your child, consider the following before starting with picture scripts:

- Is the activity enjoyable for him?
- Does he understand black and white pictures?
- Does he have the motor skills for most of the steps?
- Will he let me help him with the parts he can't do himself?
- Can he concentrate for long enough to do it?

If the answer to any of these questions is 'no', then you may need to adapt the activity to be more suitable to your child.

Could you:

- choose a more motivating activity?
- use photographs instead of line drawings if he responds better to these?
- simplify or extend the activity to suit his motor and attention skills?

3. Providing the right amount of help

Helping your child to achieve an activity independently is one of the key benefits of picture scripts. Whether this is a short-term or long-term goal will depend on the needs of your child and the activity being undertaken. More is written about this on page 15 ('Reducing adult help').

USING PICTURE SCRIPTS FOR THE FIRST TIME

Here is some guidance for getting started.

Go in easy for immediate success

It's important that your child enjoys the activity and has a positive experience of using a picture script. When you introduce the script, your primary aim should be for your child to get comfortable with it.

Think ahead!

Can you introduce the activity in a relaxed way at a time when you're not rushed, and your child is receptive to learning? If your child uses a visual timetable, make sure you let him know in advance about this new activity.

Stand back

Reflect on which steps your child can and can't do in an activity. Make sure you let your child do the parts he can already achieve independently, only providing support with the parts he finds difficult.

Getting started – step-by-step

1. Motivation.

   Show the activity to your child. Is he interested? If so, then go ahead!

   If not, then STOP! And consider a new activity (or alternatively a reward system to motivate him).

2. Show your child the script and materials.

   Tell him what you're doing, e.g. 'We're making a snowflake decoration.'

3. Look at the cover page together.

   Read the words. Then turn the page.

4. Help with the first step.

   Support your child to carry out the first step. Point to the picture. Pause to see if your child gets the right thing. If not, point to the item, and if that doesn't work, help him get the item.

5. Turn the next page.

   Tap the corner of the page, to see if your child turns it himself. Help him turn the page.

6. Continue in the same way with each step.

   Read the words and help your child to carry out the steps. Point to the pictures and the items being used.

7. Ensure fun and success for your child.

   Help your child if needed by:

   - giving him the items
   - pointing to what he needs/where things go
   - giving physical help (hand-over-hand)
   - carrying out the difficult steps yourself.

   Use lots of praise!

8. Close the book when you're finished.

Use words to make this clear, e.g. 'it's finished' or 'the end'. Clear away the materials.

REDUCING ADULT HELP

You and your child will soon be familiar with using picture scripts. However, in order to maximize your child's chance of independence, it is vital that you think about how you are currently helping, and how you can enable your child to achieve the activity on his own. Here are some examples:

- At the moment you help by turning the pages. You could help less by pointing to the corner of the page or lifting it slightly.

- You often tell your child what to do. Instead, you could just point to the picture.

- Sometimes you carry out parts of the activity for your child. You could begin doing that, pause and look at him. See if he tries himself.

- You find yourself correcting your child so he can get it just right, like the pictures in the script. Think – do you need to correct, or is his version OK? Show the child physically or point to the picture instead of using words if you need to.

MAKING YOUR OWN PICTURE SCRIPTS

The picture scripts in this book are samples to demonstrate the possibilities. You can create your own scripts for different activities you would like your child to learn or participate in. The benefit of making your own picture scripts is that you can tailor them to your child's interests and the environment.

Six steps for making your own picture scripts

1. *Identify the steps* needed to complete the activity. Be sure to include every step.

2. Check the child can understand the *type of picture* you are using (see below).

3. Use the pictures to show the *action* you want the child to learn in each step.

4. Keep the images as *simple and distraction-free* as possible. If you're taking photographs, keep the background plain white.

5. Write/type words clearly on the script. These are the words you would use to describe the action, e.g. 'Get everything ready.' *Keep the words simple.* The child may start to say the words himself when he does the activity, so consider what you would like the child to say.

6. Use a *style* of script suitable for the child and the setting (see below).

Choice of pictures

There are many types of images available, but the most important thing is the child's understanding and interest in the pictures, so be sure to establish this before you start out. Some of the options available are:

- photographs (taken by yourself, cut out of catalogues/magazines or downloaded from the internet)
- hand-drawn pictures
- picture or symbol software programmes
- clip art.

Style of scripts

The 'book style' picture scripts contained in this book have the benefit of being portable and quick to assemble. Other styles of picture script can be equally successful:

- *Single-page* picture scripts (see example on page 17) are helpful for sticking on a wall, e.g. by a sink for washing hands, and are easy to laminate.
- *Schedule-style* picture scripts, using Velcro, are familiar to many children with autism (from their visual schedules/timetables). This format enables them to remove a step when it is completed. See example on page 18.
- *Ring binders* are a flexible format for presenting picture scripts.
- A *hand-drawn list* in a notebook can be quick and effective for some students.
- *Electronic tablets* – there are an increasing range of options for presenting pictures in script format.

Make the Bed

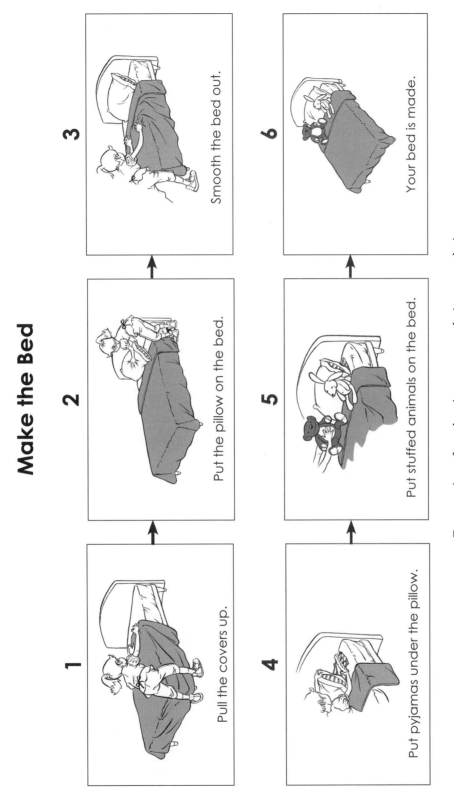

1 Pull the covers up.

2 Put the pillow on the bed.

3 Smooth the bed out.

4 Put pyjamas under the pillow.

5 Put stuffed animals on the bed.

6 Your bed is made.

Example of a single-page picture script

Toast

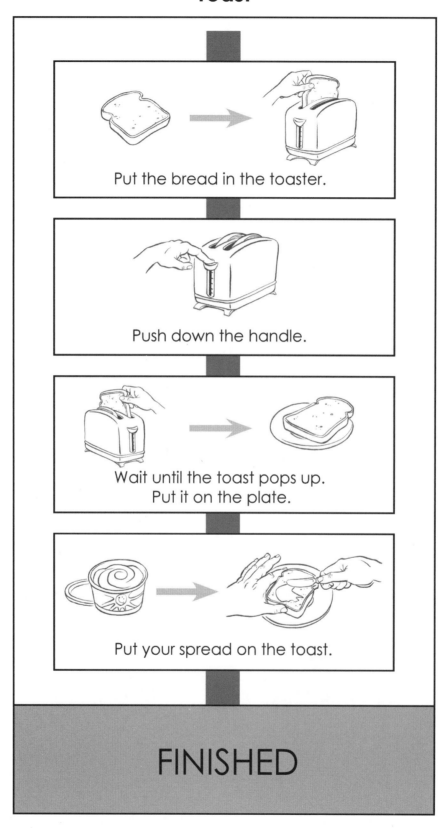

Put the bread in the toaster.

Push down the handle.

Wait until the toast pops up.
Put it on the plate.

Put your spread on the toast.

FINISHED

Example of a schedule-style picture script

PROMOTING LANGUAGE AND COMMUNICATION SKILLS

After children learn the basic skills taught with the picture scripts you can use these same picture sequences to engage in more communication and language expansion activities. Here are some tips for how to do this once your child is familiar and comfortable with an activity.

Giving instructions

- Once your child has mastered an activity, he can use the picture script as a guide to give other people instructions, step-by-step.

- It makes a nice change for your child to give an adult directions!

- If your child can read, he can read the words at each step.

- If your child uses less language, he can point to the pictures and say some words.

- This can be used as a social activity with a buddy.

- TIP: Could you try a little sabotage and get it wrong, e.g. miss out a step or choose the wrong ingredient? How does your child tell you how to do it properly?

Telling stories

- For children with conversational language skills, once you have completed an activity, you have a perfect topic of conversation!

- Look through the pictures again and talk about what you did.

- Could the child use the script later in the day to tell someone else all about it?

- TIP: If it's an activity you used with a child at school, could you send a copy of the script home in his school bag with a note to the parents, so they can talk about what he did at school?

Commenting on what's happening

- Use the script as you re-tell what the student did.

- The scripts link the words the child hears and the pictures in a concrete way that is easier for the child to understand. He can also come back to the script over and over again.

- After children learn to follow the basic picture script activities, try using those activities for expanded conversation. Try commenting on:
  - what they are doing during the activity ('You're the doctor!')
  - what the activity is ('We're drawing a tree')
  - what is next ('Time for a curved piece now')
  - what just happened ('That marble went down really fast!')
  - their achievements ('Well done, you gave her lovely long hair!')

- emotional states ('You're smiling because you're happy – you like Mr Potato Head').
- Encourage the child to use more language by modelling what they could say and pausing to give them a chance to copy, e.g. point to the picture script and say 'He has a red nose.' Then point to Mr Potato Head and say, 'He has…[pause] a red nose.'

Asking and answering questions

- Picture script activities provide familiar structured opportunities for children to practise this skill.
- The picture scripts help provide a focus to develop your child's concentration for dealing with more complex questions.
- Be careful not to ask too many questions, otherwise you may spoil the child's enjoyment and motivation.
- Here are some types of questions you could try:
  - *About the activity (here-and-now)* – 'Where is the flashlight?'
  - *About the child (here-and-now)* – 'There's Mr Potato Head's hat. Does it fit your head?'
  - *About the child (more abstract)* – 'The cat's finished! Have you got a pet?'
  - *General (abstract)* – 'There's the fish's eye. What do we do with our eyes?'
  - *Other people* – 'What would Mrs Bowyer say if we burnt the toast?'
  - *Solving problems* – 'Uh-oh, we don't have any pink icing, what shall we do?'
- Not all children will be able to answer questions, and if you find that this is too hard for your child, then offer choices instead, e.g. 'do *we see* or *hear* with our eyes?'
- If your child is very good at answering questions, try role reversal, and see if he can practise asking you questions while you carry out the activity.

PICTURE SCRIPTS FOR OLDER STUDENTS

The scripts in this book target the needs of younger children. Picture scripts continue to be useful for older students and adults with autism, as they will continue to benefit from the visual approach and the structure provided by the picture scripts. The same principles apply regarding making the scripts, but activities should be tailored to the individual's differing motivations and needs. For instance, the games would be played with age-appropriate toys/characters. There may also be more of a focus on wider life skills, such as going to the (real) supermarket or making a cup of coffee.

NOTE

In this book, for ease of reading, the authors use the pronouns 'he' and 'him' when referring to a child with autism.

Chapter 2

PRETEND PLAY

INTRODUCTION

During pretend play, children typically learn about their world, the people around them and themselves. Pretending can sometimes be hard for children with autism because it involves paying attention to what other people do and using their imagination. Pretend play can be difficult for them. In spite of this they can still develop skills in this area. This chapter contains seven picture scripts examples for some simple concrete pretend play scenarios seen in various forms in classrooms and homes across the world.

Picture scripts are useful tools for helping children with autism begin to learn to use pretend play toys such as toy food or a doctor's kit. Sometimes children are already interested in these toys but they get 'stuck' playing with them in a particular way. A picture script will give them new ideas about how to play.

Several of the picture scripts in this chapter involve more than one person, which can create opportunities for your child to play with another child. Sometimes it can be beneficial for your child to 'practise' with an adult so they are familiar with a game or activity before involving another child. If your child plays with other children who use the toys or do the activities in a different way from the scripts, you may need to adjust the scripts to match their play patterns.

Enjoy playing!

Play
Cars

P1

Get the cars.

P2

Start the engine. 'Vroom vroom.'

P3

Make it go FAST.

P4

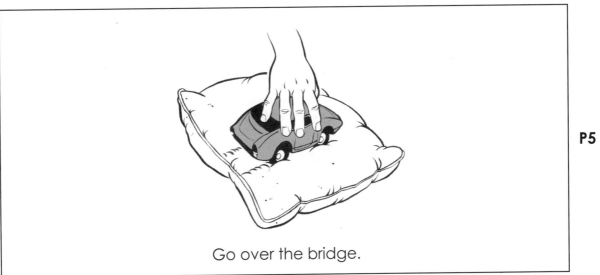

Go over the bridge.

P5

Go through the tunnel. 'Beep beep.'

P6

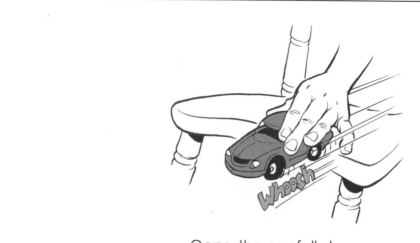

Oops, the car fell down.

They go CRASH!

Here come the police.
'WHEEEEOOOO WHEEEEOOOO WHEEEEOOOO.'

Racing the cars.

Going round a track.

P10

Other ideas to try:

Go Shopping

P1

Make a list.

P2

Get a basket.

P3

P4

Fill your basket up.

P5

Go to the checkout.

P6

Put your items on the counter.

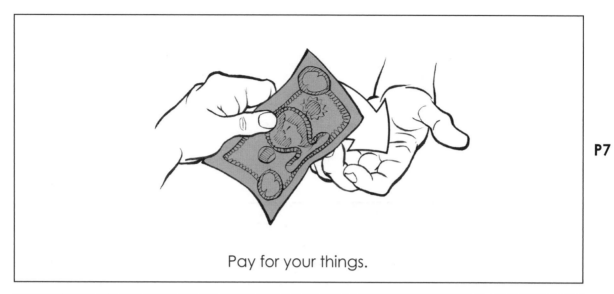

Pay for your things.

P7

Pack your bags.

P8

Tea Party

P1

Cups

Teapot

Teaspoon

Plates

Sugar bowl

Toy food

Get everything out.

P2

'A cup for me and a cup for you.'

P3

Pour the tea.

P4

Add some sugar.

P5

Drink your tea. 'Hmmm.'

P6

Have a cookie!

P7

Give some tea to teddy.

Eat some cake.

Mop up a spill.

Other things to do at your tea party:

P8

Dolly's
Bath

P1

| Dolly | Bath/bowl | Sponge | Towel |

Get everything out.

P2

Get the bath ready.

P3

P4

Take off dolly's clothes.

P5

Put dolly in the bath.

P6

Wash dolly's body.

Clean dolly's face.

P7

Wash dolly's hair.

P8

Put dolly on the towel.

P9

COPYRIGHT © SIMONE GRIFFIN, RUTH HARRIS AND LINDA HODGDON 2013

Dry her off.

P10

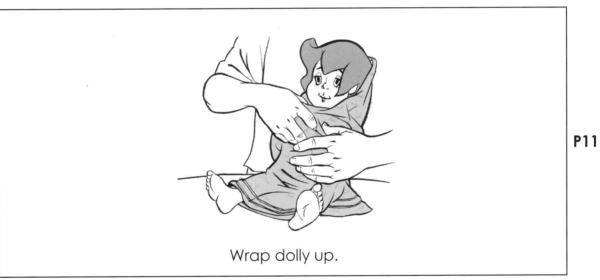

Wrap dolly up.

P11

Rock dolly to sleep.

P12

Bus Game

P1

Line up some chairs.

P2

Make pretend wheels with cushions.

P3

Sit down in the chairs.

P4

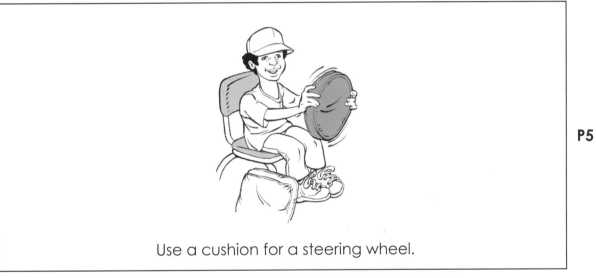

Use a cushion for a steering wheel.

P5

Sing the 'Wheels on the Bus' song.

P6

Use your hands to show the wheels going round.

P7

Use your hands to show the wipers.

P8

Stand up and down.

P9

SCRIPT 2.6 **CUBBIES AND DENS**

Cubbies and Dens

P1

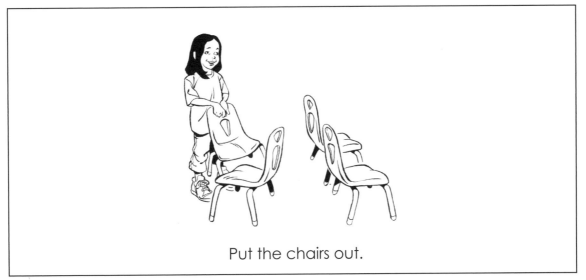

Put the chairs out.

P2

Cover the chairs.

P3

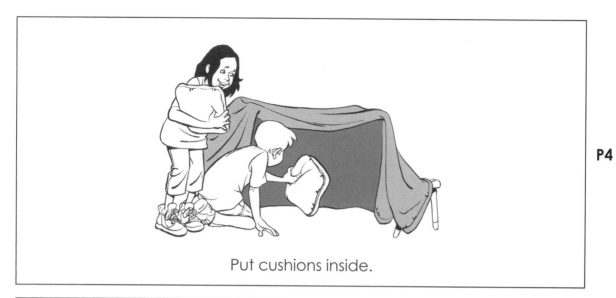

Put cushions inside.

P4

Get some toys.

P5

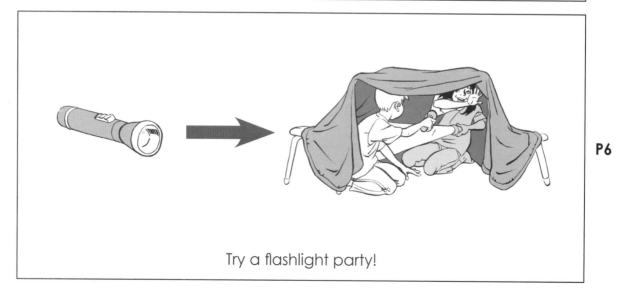

Try a flashlight party!

P6

Play
Doctors

P1

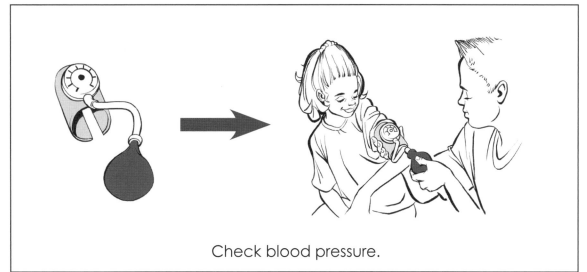

Open your medical kit.

P2

Check blood pressure.

P3

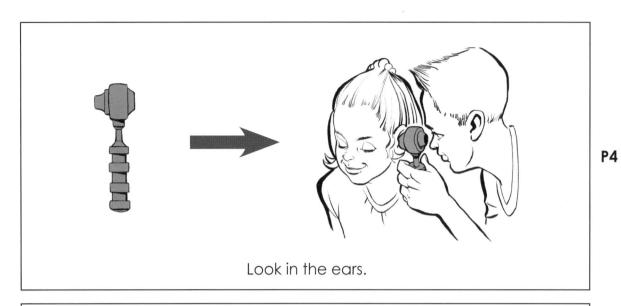

Look in the ears.

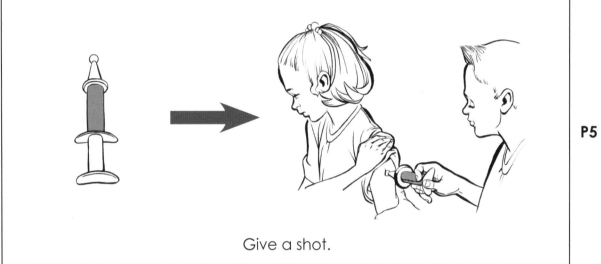

Give a shot.

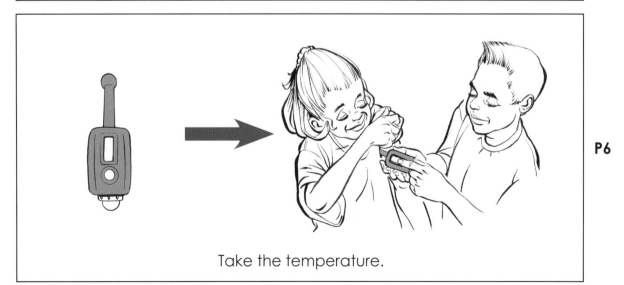

Take the temperature.

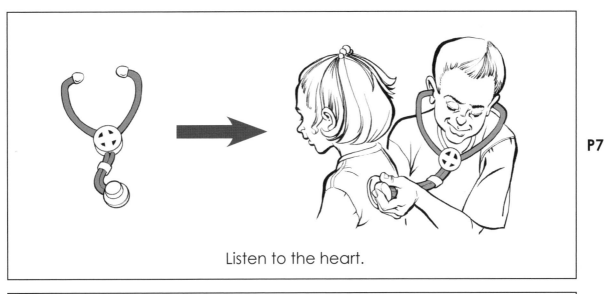

Listen to the heart.

P7

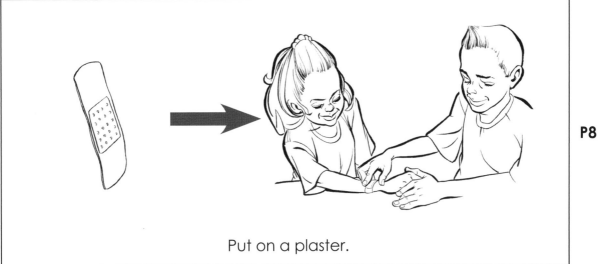

Put on a plaster.

P8

All better. 'Good-bye!'

P9

Chapter 3

DRAWING PICTURES

INTRODUCTION

Those first colourful drawings, proudly brought home from school and stuck up on the fridge door, are something that parents treasure long after their children are grown up. Some children with autism are very talented artists, having an eye for logos and patterns they see around them and then faithfully recreating the images themselves. For other children with autism, learning to draw a simple picture is made possible by working through picture scripts step-by-step. It can almost seem like magic when a girl or boy, who has never produced a picture before, is independently drawing pictures with the help of a picture script within the space of a few days or weeks.

The eight drawing scripts included here, from easiest through to most advanced, have been carefully selected. Some children quickly learn to draw using picture scripts, in which case you could find that they move swiftly from a tree to a steam train! The house, flower and tree images can be added to one page to make a traditional composite picture, though another combination altogether may appeal to your child – a fish riding a dinosaur, perhaps?

Colouring in their picture scripts provides an excellent opportunity for your child to become interested in colours. The different options at end of the 'Face' picture script enable you to make the script more advanced for a child who likes a challenge.

As with all the picture scripts included in this book, the ideas for drawings are designed as a sample to appeal to as wide a range of children as possible. Once your child has acquired the skills to follow the picture scripts in this book, you can expand the activity by finding pictures from other sources. The internet is an amazing resource for learning how to construct simple drawings. So if your child would love to know how to draw Smurfs, Teletubbies, Disney characters or whatever it may be, then a Google search is likely to bring up something useful for you.

Happy drawing!

SCRIPT 3.1 DRAW A TREE

Draw
a Tree

P1

Draw the tree trunk.

P2

Draw the leaves.

P3

Draw some grass.

Colour it in.

SCRIPT 3.2 DRAW A FACE

Draw
a Face

P1

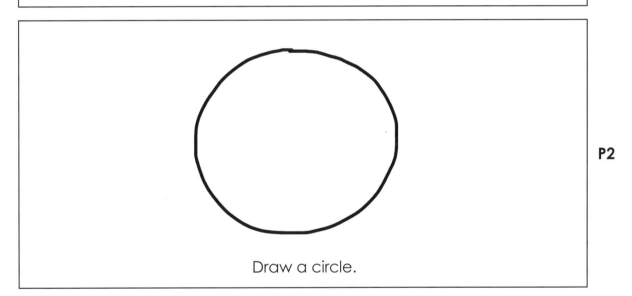

Draw a circle.

P2

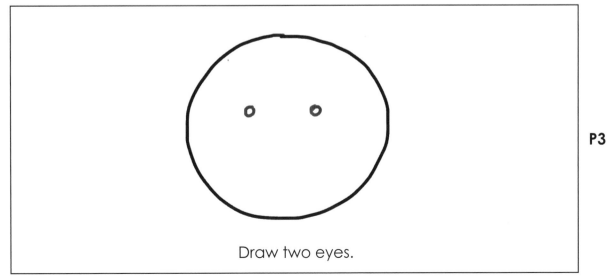

Draw two eyes.

P3

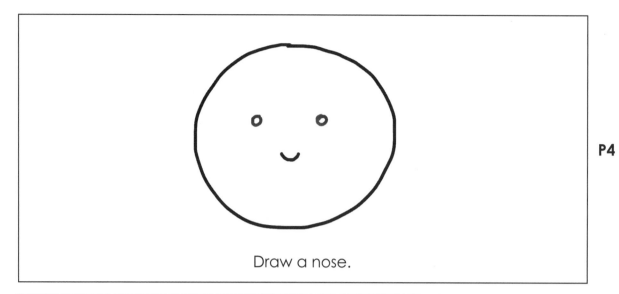

P4

Draw a nose.

P5

Draw a mouth.

P6

Draw some hair.

Try different types of hair.

P7

Draw
a House

P1

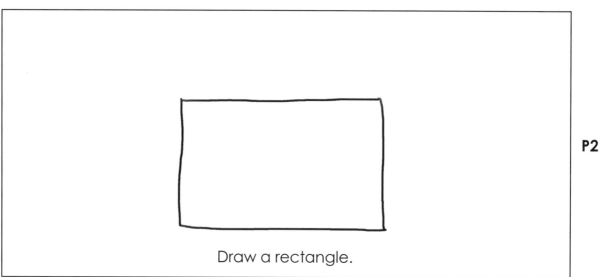

Draw a rectangle.

P2

Draw a roof.

P3

Draw the windows.

P4

Draw a door.

P5

Draw a chimney.

P6

Colour it in.

SCRIPT 3.4   DRAW A FISH

Draw
a Fish

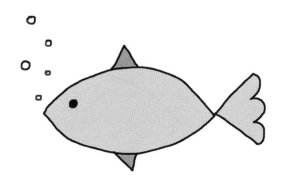

P1

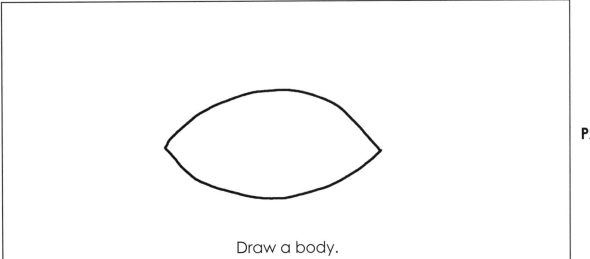

Draw a body.

P2

Draw a tail.

P3

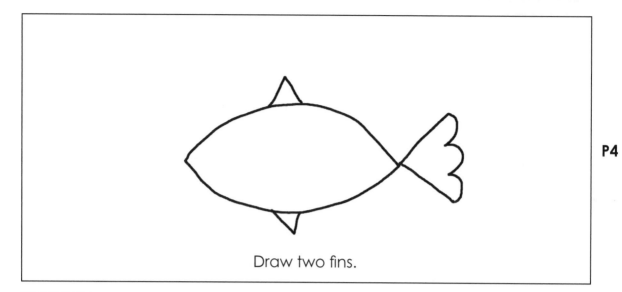

Draw two fins.

P4

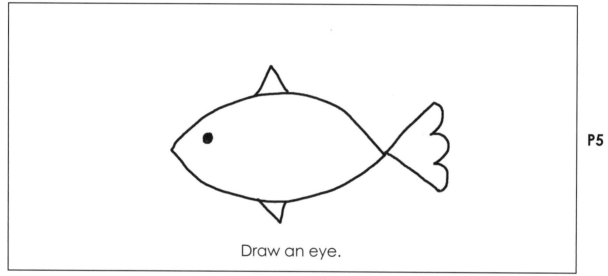

Draw an eye.

P5

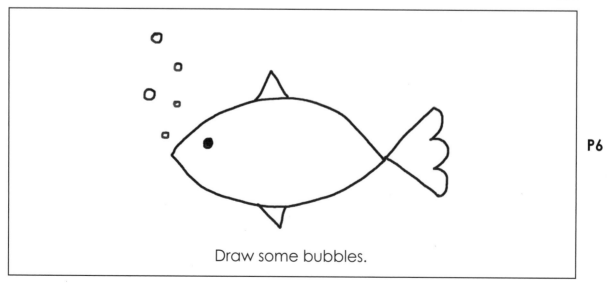

Draw some bubbles.

P6

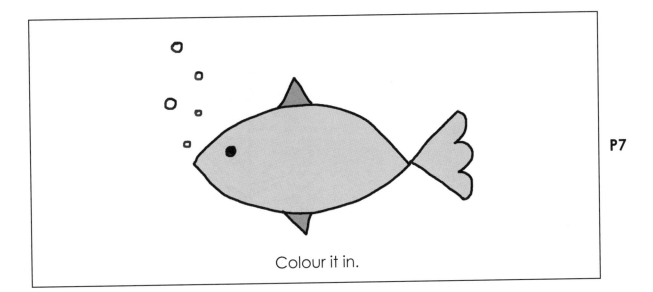

Colour it in.

P7

Draw
a Flower

P1

○

Draw a circle.

P2

Draw a stem.

P3

Draw petals.

P4

Draw leaves.

P5

Colour it in.

P6

Draw
a Monster

P1

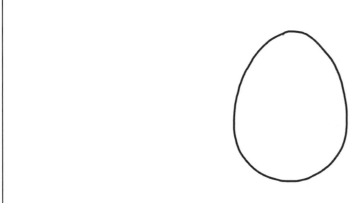

Draw a body.

P2

Draw legs and feet.

P3

Draw arms and hands.

P4

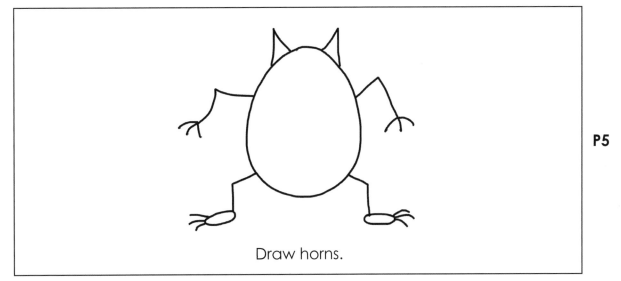

Draw horns.

P5

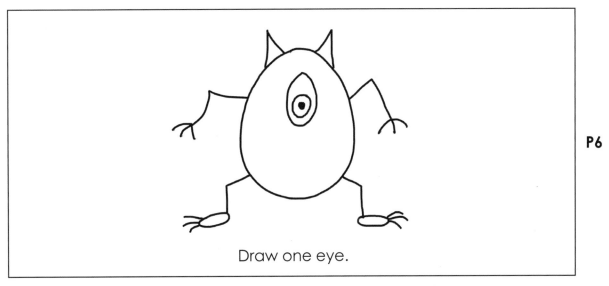

Draw one eye.

P6

Draw a mouth and teeth.

P7

Colour it in.

P8

SCRIPT 3.7   **DRAW A DINOSAUR**

Draw
a Dinosaur

P1

Draw the body.

P2

Draw the head.

P3

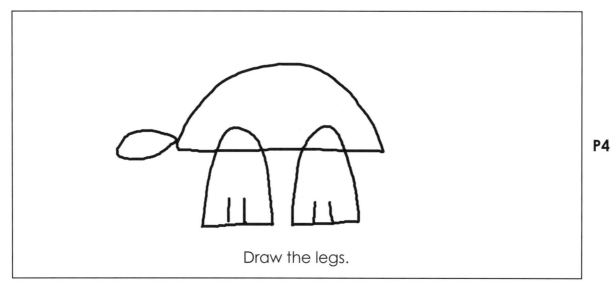

Draw the legs.

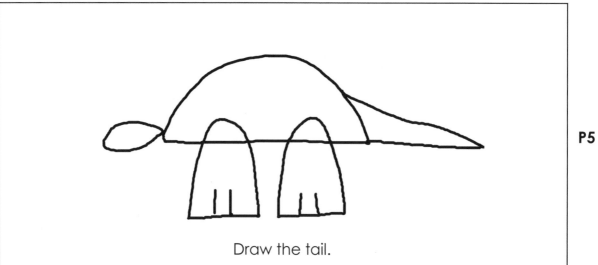

Draw the tail.

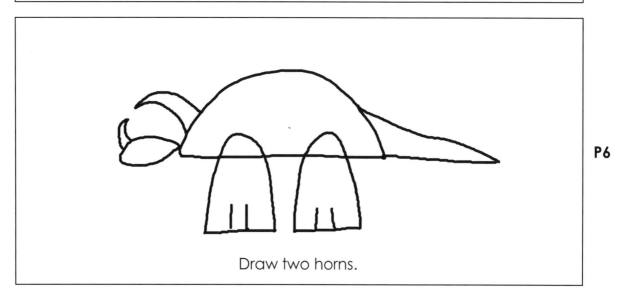

Draw two horns.

Draw some spikes.

P7

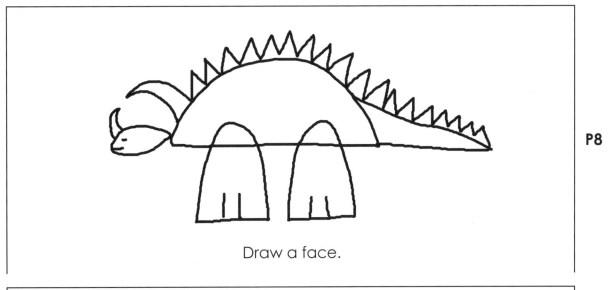

Draw a face.

P8

Colour it in.

P9

Draw a Steam
Train

P1

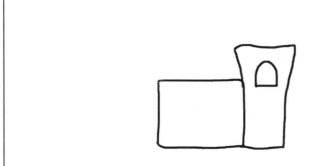

Draw a rectangle.

P2

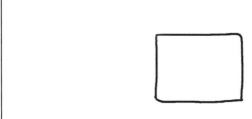

Draw a cab.

P3

Draw wheels and a piston.

P4

Draw a chimney and steam.

P5

Draw a carriage.

P6

Draw some windows.

Draw some wheels.

Draw a light and whistle.

Draw a train track.

P10

Colour it in.

P11

Chapter 4

BUILDING AND CONSTRUCTION GAMES

INTRODUCTION

Coming up with original ideas during play can be tough for children with autism. This can make it hard for them to occupy themselves with simple building and construction activities – like LEGO, wooden blocks or playdough – in the way their peers can. If they learn more things to do with the construction tools, they will be better able to join in with other children playing with these toys.

For teachers and parents this can be a challenge. You want to help them to make something nice, but how often have you been the one who has ended up 'taking over' and putting together the Mr Potato Head or playdough animal for the child? Often children with autism have the motor skills to put the pieces together, but find it tricky to know *what* to make, so the picture scripts in this section have some fun and simple ideas for children to follow (with just a bit of help from you to get them started). This will help them achieve something really satisfying in the final result.

One of the exciting things about these building and construction activities is the opportunity to extend them once they're mastered. Maybe the little boy who loves LEGO, but has been unable to make anything that satisfies him (so he resorts to emptying the box each time in frustration), can now have the chance to sit with other kids around the toy box while he makes an aeroplane. Then you've got a basis to help develop his pretend play skills. (Perhaps you could write another script about how to play with the aeroplane?) Or the little girl who wants to join in with the others, but is still developing early turn-taking skills – maybe if she learns to build a marble run using a script, she can enjoy rolling the balls down with another child?

These examples should give you some ideas of your own. Use these picture scripts as models to develop your own scripts using different materials such as wooden blocks, train sets, cardboard boxes or Stickle Bricks.

Happy building!

SCRIPT 4.1   SAND CASTLE

Sand Castle

P1

Sand   Bucket   Shovel   Water

You will need:

P2

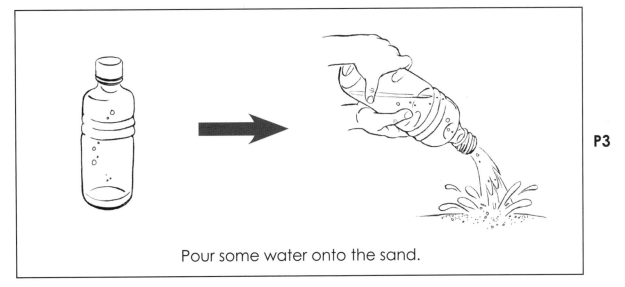

Pour some water onto the sand.

P3

Put the wet sand into the bucket.

P4

Push the sand down.

P5

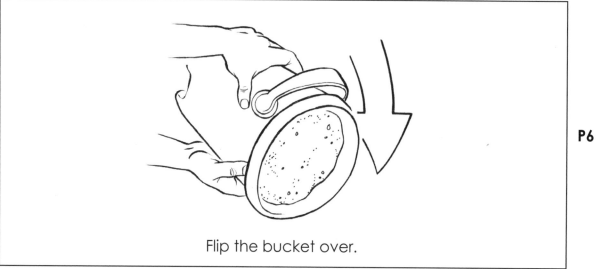

Flip the bucket over.

P6

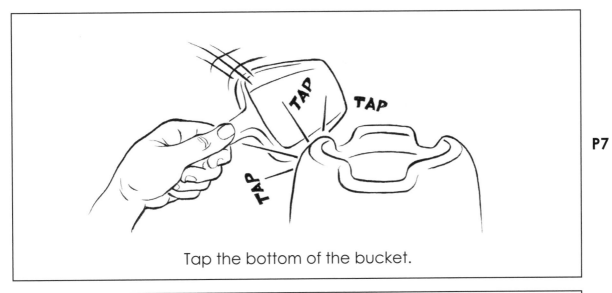

Tap the bottom of the bucket.

P7

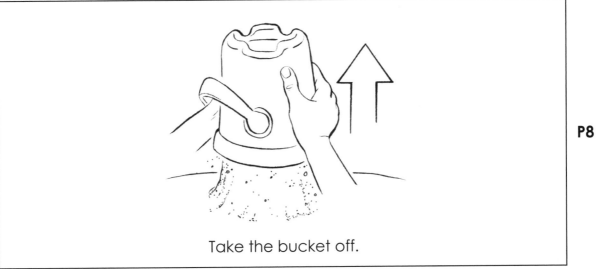

Take the bucket off.

P8

Well done! You have made a sand castle.

P9

Decorate your
sand castle.

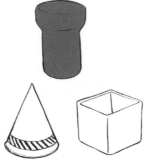

Use different
containers.

Make lots of sand
castles.

P10

Other ideas you could try:

SCRIPT 4.2   PLAYDOUGH CATERPILLAR

Playdough Caterpillar

P1

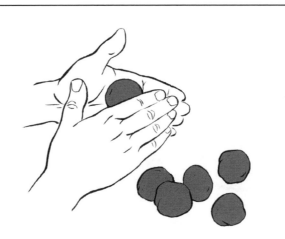

Make 6 little balls.

P2

Push the balls together to make the body.

P3

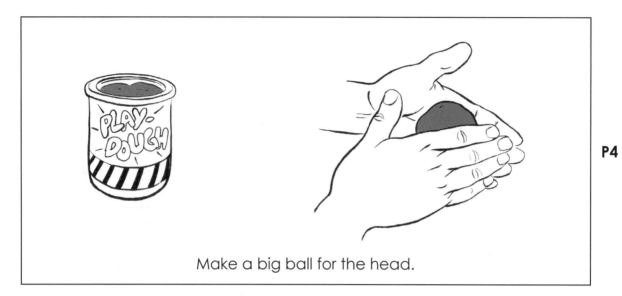

Make a big ball for the head.

P4

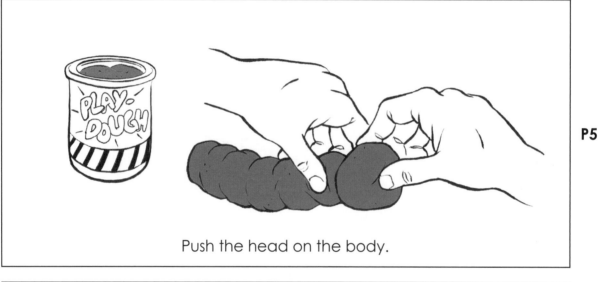

Push the head on the body.

P5

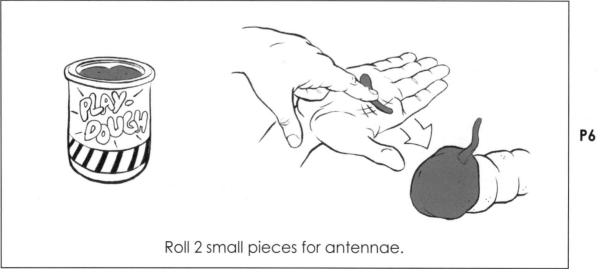

Roll 2 small pieces for antennae.

P6

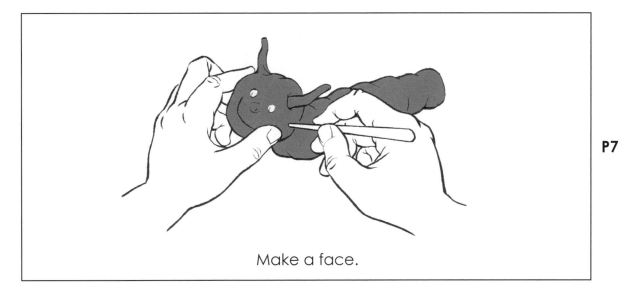

Make a face.

P7

Your caterpillar is finished.

P8

Snail   Face   Birthday cake

What else could you make?

P9

Mr Potato Head

P1

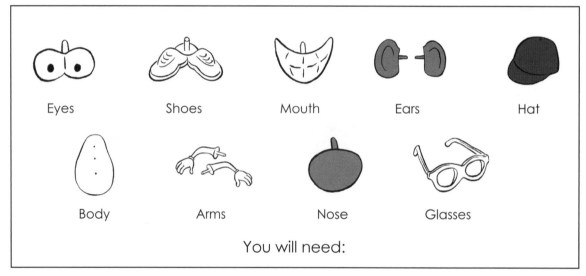

Eyes   Shoes   Mouth   Ears   Hat

Body   Arms   Nose   Glasses

You will need:

P2

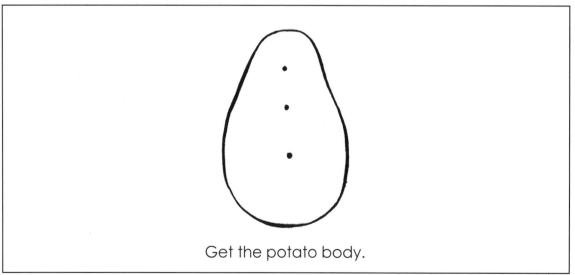

Get the potato body.

P3

Put on his shoes.

P4

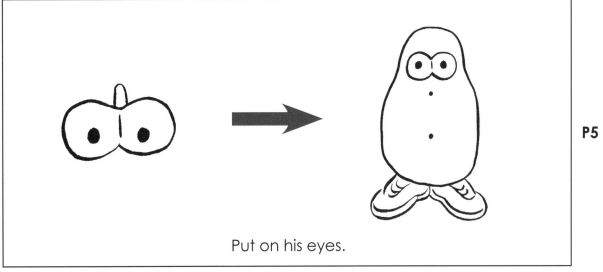

Put on his eyes.

P5

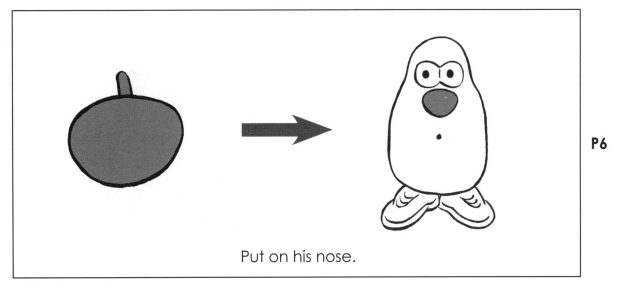

Put on his nose.

P6

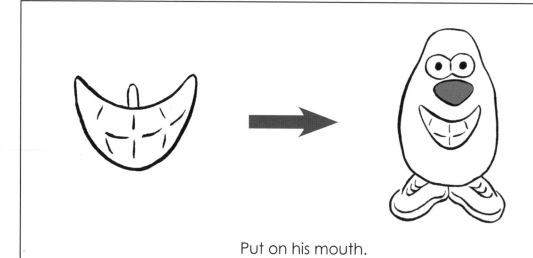

Put on his mouth.

P7

Put on his ears.

P8

Put on his arms.

P9

Put on his hat.

P10

Put on his glasses.

P11

Mr Potato Head is finished.

P12

| Make him look silly. | Make him talk. | Use different pieces. |

Other things to do with Mr Potato Head:

P13

SCRIPT 4.4 MARBLE RUN

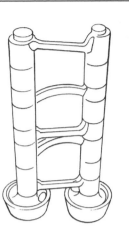

Marble Run

P1

Straight pieces   Curved pieces   Marbles

P2

Base pieces   Small pieces   Special piece

You will need:

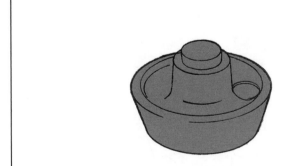 

Get two base pieces.

P3

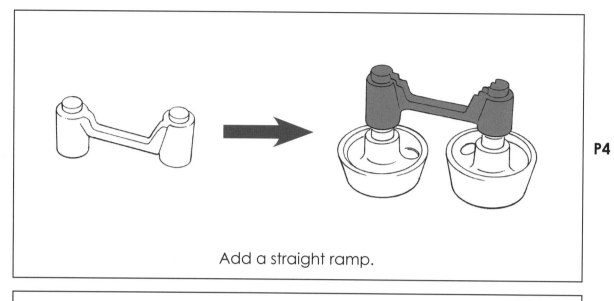

P4

Add a straight ramp.

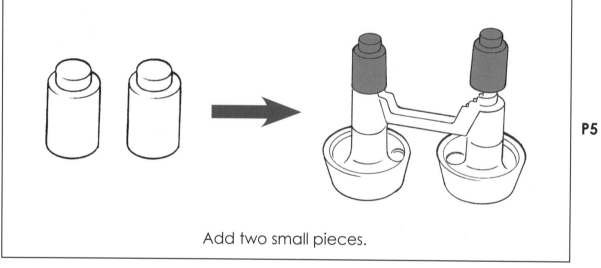

P5

Add two small pieces.

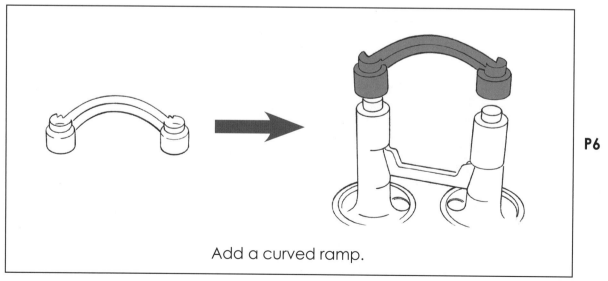

P6

Add a curved ramp.

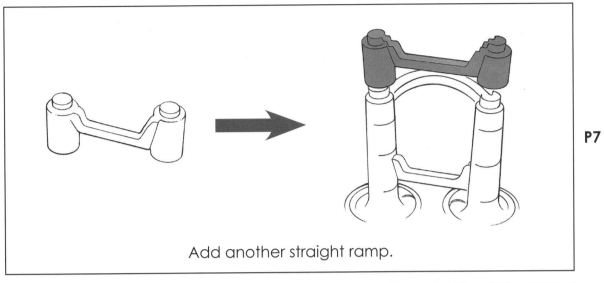

P7

Add another straight ramp.

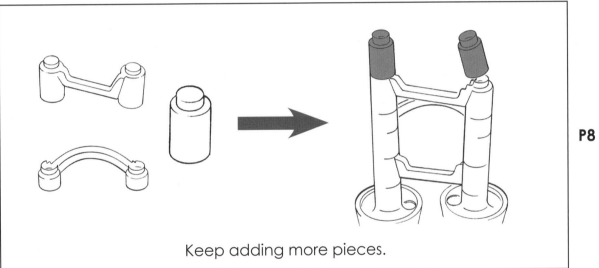

P8

Keep adding more pieces.

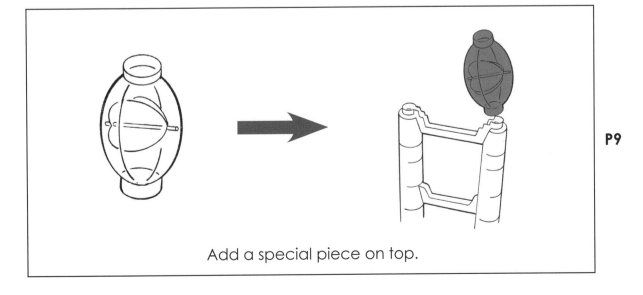

P9

Add a special piece on top.

Drop the marbles in the top.

P10

Take turns if someone else wants to play.

P11

LEGO Plane

P1

Get the LEGO out.

P2

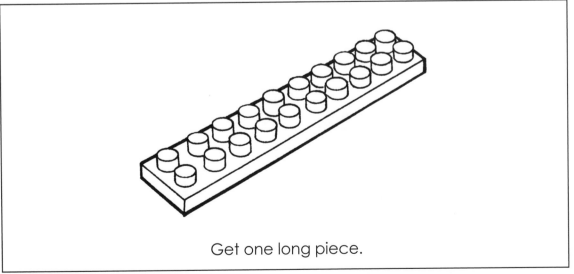

Get one long piece.

P3

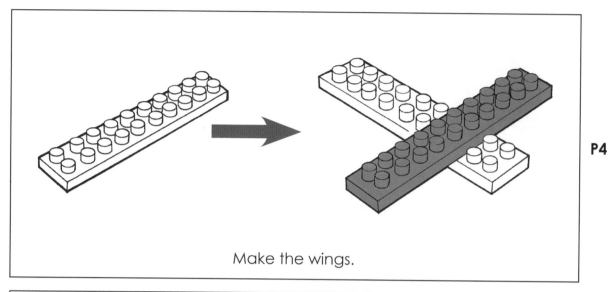

Make the wings.

P4

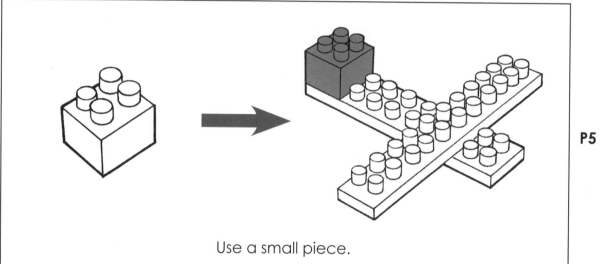

Use a small piece.

P5

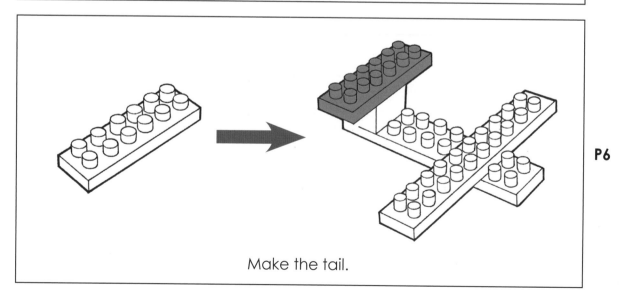

Make the tail.

P6

P7

Turn the plane over.

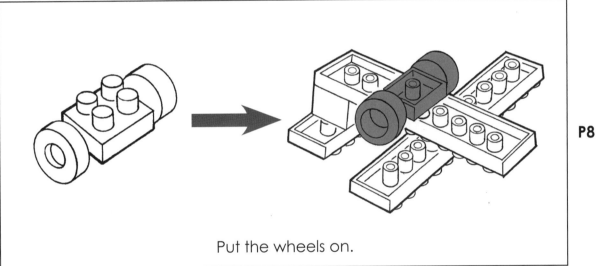

P8

Put the wheels on.

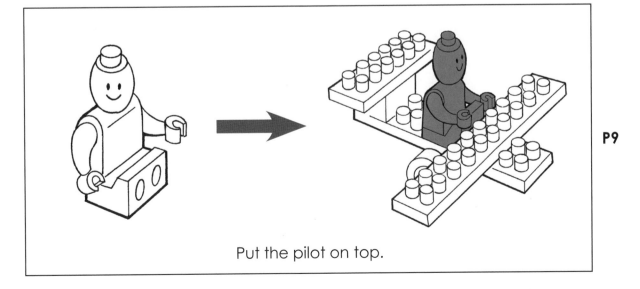

P9

Put the pilot on top.

Ready for take off!

Chapter 5

COOKING

INTRODUCTION

Most children love to cook – it's fun to do and even nicer to eat something tasty at the end. When teaching children with autism to cook, it's all too easy to dive in early to help. If you're tempted to do this, then remember that one of the most useful life skills your child can learn is being able to prepare themselves a simple meal or snack.

With this in mind, we have included some practical scripts that will help your child to develop some life-long skills and some fun ideas to keep them motivated.

Of course kitchens contain lots of hazards; hot ovens and sharp knives for a start. That makes this chapter of the book different from others, because adult supervision is required to a varying extent for many of the recipes. It's a skilful balance as the supervising adult to keep the child safe whilst genuinely enabling them to develop their independence. To help you with this, we've used a symbol to highlight the most obvious places where there are hazards during the cooking activities. This can also be used to enable the children to develop their skills in asking for help.

These scripts are some of the most advanced in the book. You only realize what a complex task cooking is when you try to make it simple! There are many choices involved – for instance, popcorn flavourings and pizza toppings. We have added picture choice boards for the most common ingredients in each recipe. These can be used to aid some children to choose and communicate to you what they want to add to the recipes. If you are using different ingredients you can add your own choice board with pictures to represent your additional ingredients.

On a practical note, laminating the pictures that will be used in the kitchen will help them last longer with all those sticky fingers around.

Happy cooking!

Toast

P1

Bread   Spreads   Butter   Toaster   Knife   Plate

Get everything out.

P2

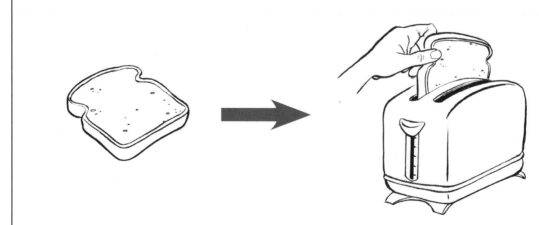

Put the bread in the toaster.

P3

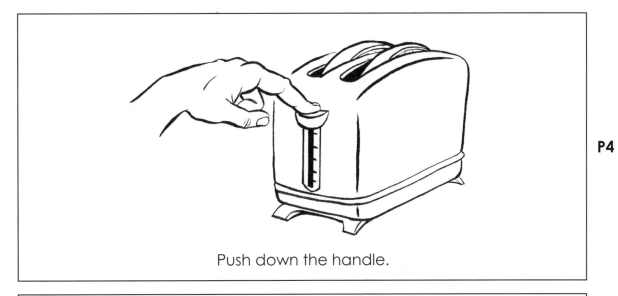

Push down the handle.

P4

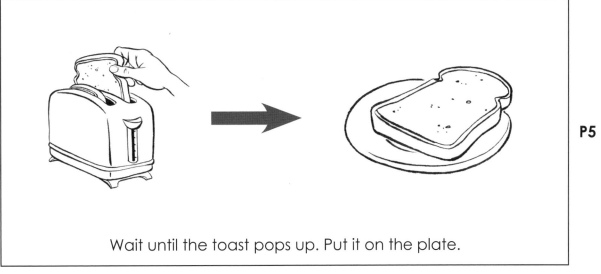

Wait until the toast pops up. Put it on the plate.

P5

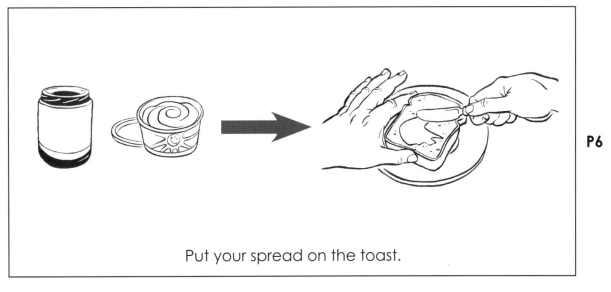

Put your spread on the toast.

P6

Eat your toast.

P7

| Butter | Peanut butter | Jam/jelly | Spreads |
| Cinnamon sugar | Chocolate spread | Cheese | |

Choice board: toast

P8

Sandwich

P1

Bread

Fillings

Butter

Plate

Knife

P2

Get everything out.

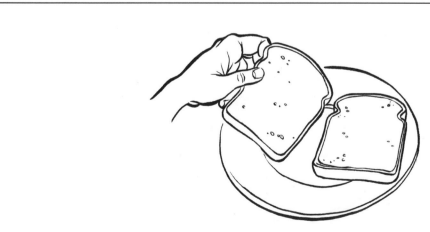

P3

Put two slices of bread on a plate.

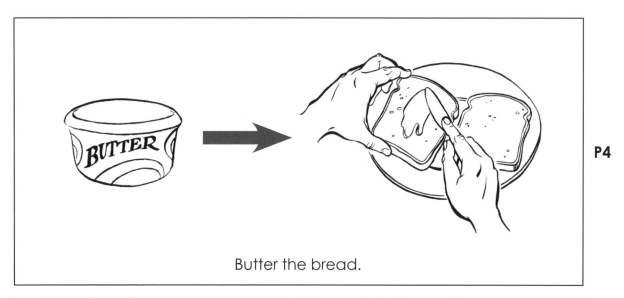

Butter the bread.

P4

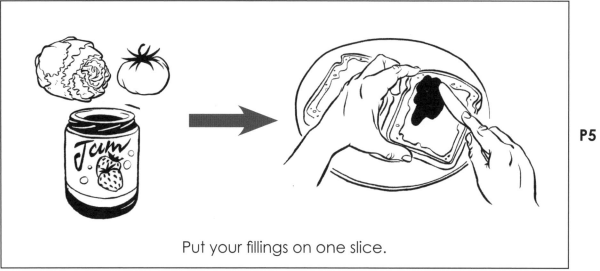

Put your fillings on one slice.

P5

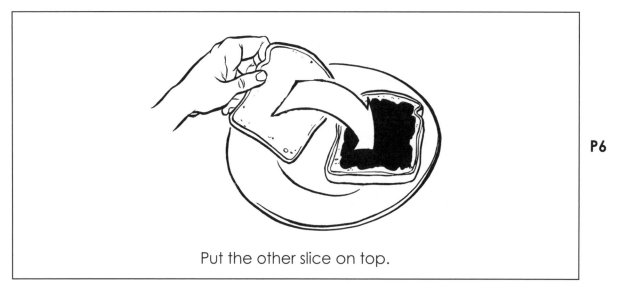

Put the other slice on top.

P6

Cut the sandwich in half.

P7

Eat your sandwich.

P8

| Meat | Jam/jelly | Tomato | Lettuce |
| Spreads | Cheese | Peanut butter | Egg |

Choice board: sandwich

P9

Ice Cream
Soda

P1

Soda/fizzy drink	Ice cream	Spoon	Glass
		Straw	

Get everything out.

P2

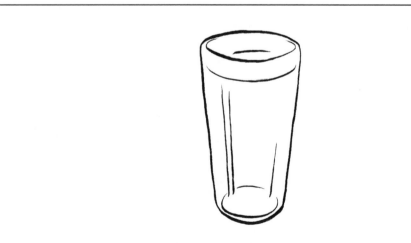

Get your glass ready.

P3

P4

Put two scoops of ice cream in the glass.

P5

Pour in some soda/fizzy drink.

P6

Watch your ice cream soda grow!

Get ready to drink quickly.

SCRIPT 5.4   FRUIT SMOOTHIE

Fruit
Smoothie

P1

| Milk | Honey | Fruit | Blender | Glass |

Get everything out.

P2

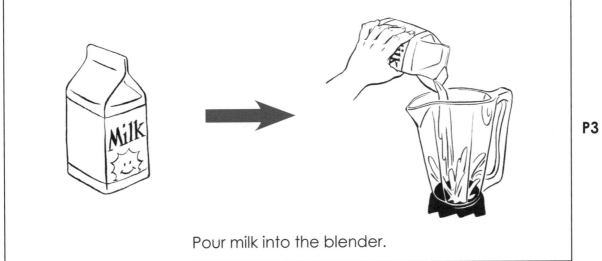

Pour milk into the blender.

P3

Put fruit into the blender.

P4

Add some honey.

P5

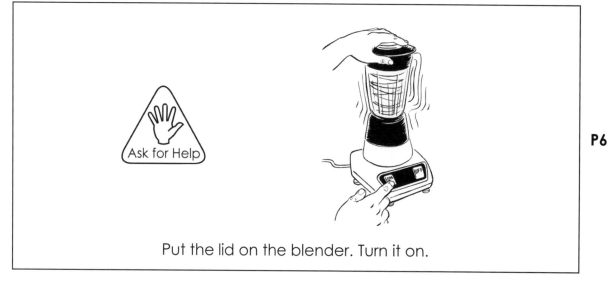

Put the lid on the blender. Turn it on.

P6

When the smoothie is ready, turn the blender off.

P7

Pour it into a glass.

P8

Drink your fruit smoothie.

P9

✓

Banana	Strawberries	Berries	Ice cream	Yoghurt

P10

Choice board: fruit smoothie

102   COPYRIGHT © SIMONE GRIFFIN, RUTH HARRIS AND LINDA HODGDON 2013

Mini Pizza

P1

Toppings	Pizza sauce	Tray	Knife
Grated cheese	Muffins	Spatula	Plate

Get everything out.

P2

Ask for Help

SET / OFF   F   180

P3

Turn the oven on to 180 degrees C (400 degrees F).

Cut a muffin open. Put them on the tray.

P4

Put some sauce on the muffins.

P5

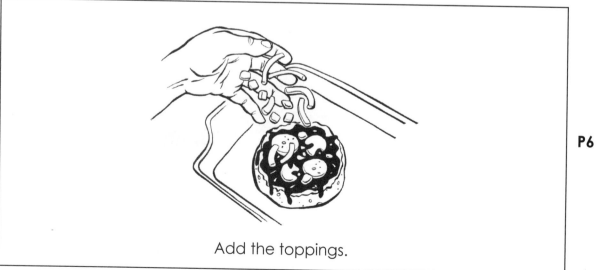

Add the toppings.

P6

Put some cheese on top.

P7

Ask an adult to put the mini pizzas in the oven.

P8

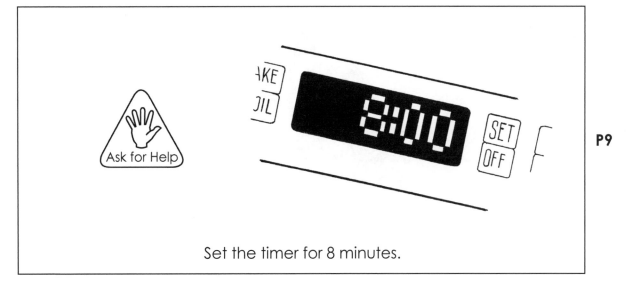

Set the timer for 8 minutes.

P9

When the timer goes off, ask an adult to take them out.

P10

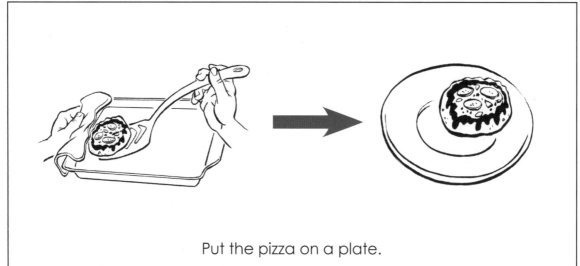

Put the pizza on a plate.

P11

Eat your pizza.

P12

P13

Choice board: mini pizza

Nachos

P1

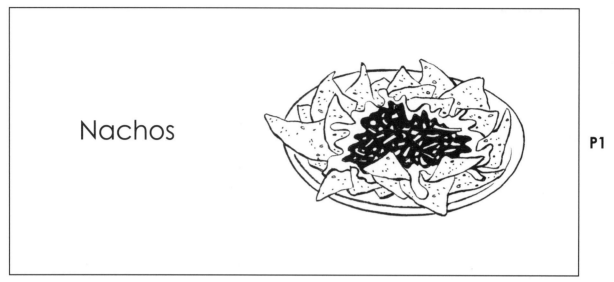

| Corn chips | Grated cheese | Toppings | Plate | Spoon |

Get everything out.

P2

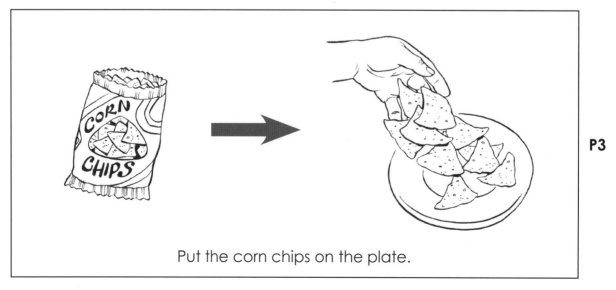

Put the corn chips on the plate.

P3

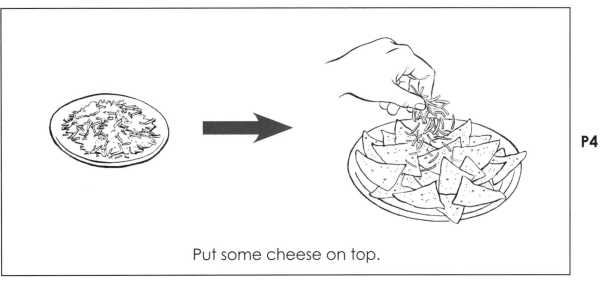

Put some cheese on top.

P4

Put the plate in the microwave and close the door.

P5

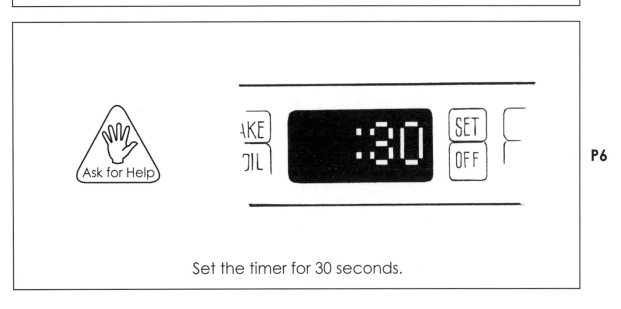

Set the timer for 30 seconds.

P6

P7

Take out the plate.

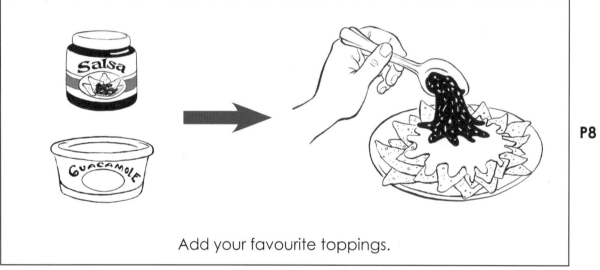

P8

Add your favourite toppings.

P9

Share your nachos with your friends.

P10

Salsa Guacamole Sour cream Sweetcorn

Choice board: nachos

Fruit and Marshmallow Salad

P1

Marshmallows   Fruit

Bowl   Spoons

Knife   Chopping board

Get everything out.

P2

Wash the fruit gently.

P3

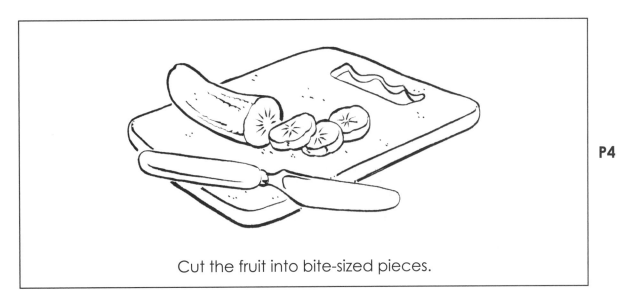

Cut the fruit into bite-sized pieces.

P4

Put the fruit into the bowl.

P5

Put some marshmallows in the bowl.

P6

Use the spoons to mix it up.

P7

Fruit and marshmallow kebabs

Something else you could make:

P8

Banana	Grapes	Apple
Strawberry	Orange	Melon

Choice board: fruit

P9

Popcorn

P1

Popcorn   Toppings   Bowl   Paper bag   Spoon

Get everything out.

P2

Put 3 spoons of popcorn in the bag.

P3

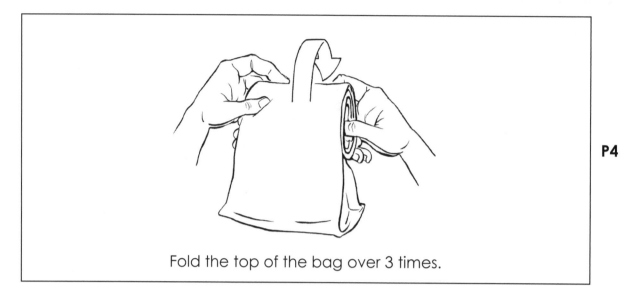

Fold the top of the bag over 3 times.

P4

Put the bag in the microwave.

P5

Ask for Help

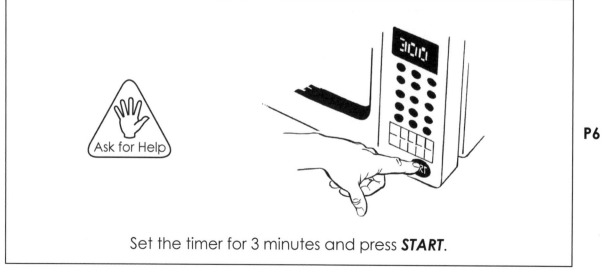

Set the timer for 3 minutes and press **START**.

P6

 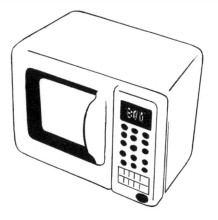

Listen to the popping noise. When the popping stops, turn the microwave off.

P7

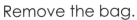

Remove the bag.

P8

Open the bag and let the steam out.

P9

Put the popcorn in a bowl.

Add your favourite topping.

Share your popcorn.

P10

P11

P12

Butter

Salt/seasoning

Icing
(powdered) sugar

P13

Choice board: popcorn

Funny Face Cookies

P1

Water	Cookies	Candy/sweets	Spoon	Plate

Icing sugar	Food colouring	Bowl	Knife

Get everything out.

P2

Put some icing sugar in the bowl.

P3

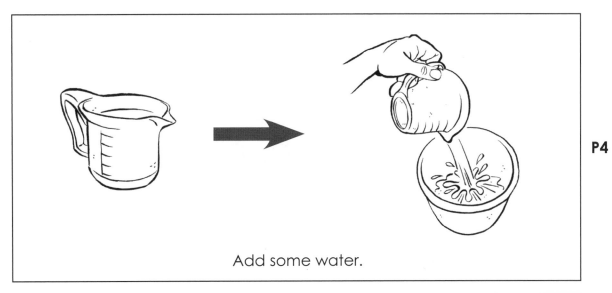

Add some water.

P4

Mix it together.

P5

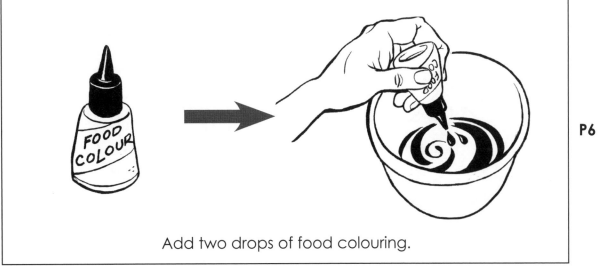

Add two drops of food colouring.

P6

Stir the icing.

P7

Put a cookie on the plate.

P8

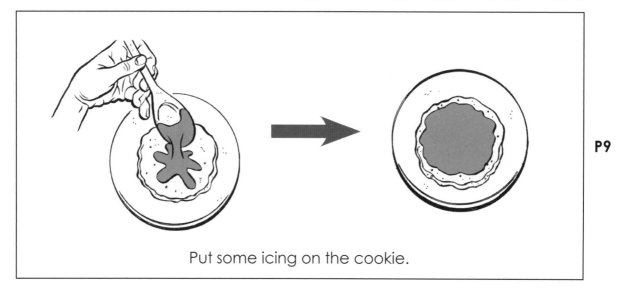

Put some icing on the cookie.

P9

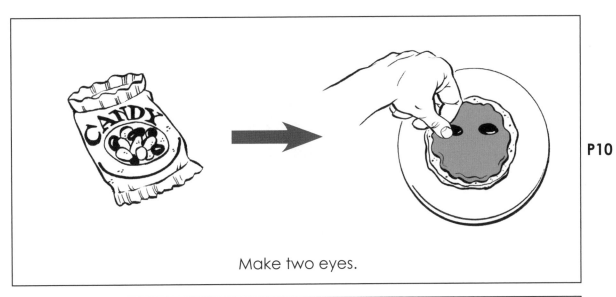

Make two eyes.

P10

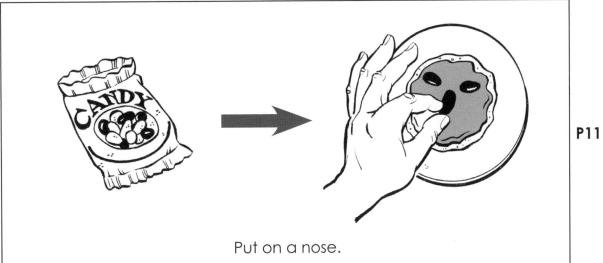

Put on a nose.

P11

Add a candy mouth.

P12

Your funny face cookie is finished.

P13

Eat your cookie.

P14

SCRIPT 5.10 CUPCAKES

Cupcakes

P1

| Self-raising (all-purpose) flour | Eggs | Cupcake tray | Bowl | Beater |
| Sugar | Soft butter | Paper cases | ½ cup measure |

Get everything out.

P2

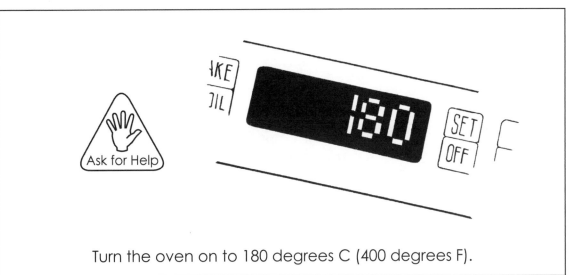

Ask for Help

Turn the oven on to 180 degrees C (400 degrees F).

P3

Put paper cases in the tray.

P4

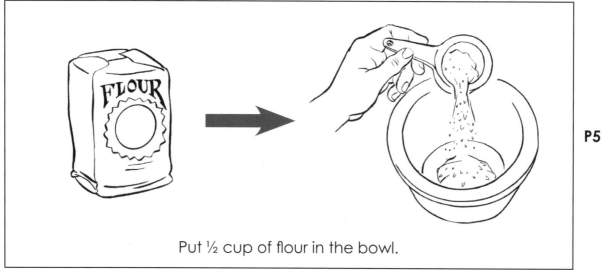

Put ½ cup of flour in the bowl.

P5

Put ½ cup of sugar in the bowl.

P6

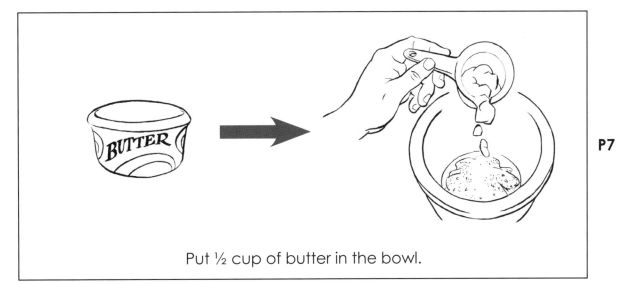

Put ½ cup of butter in the bowl.

P7

Crack two eggs into the bowl.

P8

Ask for Help

Mix everything together.

P9

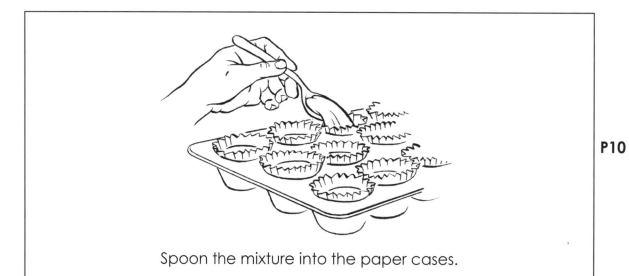

Spoon the mixture into the paper cases.

P10

Ask an adult to put them in the oven.

P11

Set the timer for 10 minutes.

P12

When timer goes off, ask an adult to take them out.

P13

Take them out of the tray. Let them cool.

P14

Share your cupcakes.

P15

Chapter 6

ARTS AND CRAFTS

INTRODUCTION

Simple arts and crafts activities can be fun additions to the classroom. They provide lots of opportunities for children with autism to learn how to plan, experiment and create something special. Children love having something to take home and show mum or dad, or to use at school for 'Show and Tell'.

You can help children decide what to make by preparing real examples, or you can simply show them some pictures from the scripts. Giving them a choice will help maintain their motivation. Like the 'Cooking' chapter, the first page in these arts and crafts picture scripts show the children what they need to get ready before they start. This is designed to help them organize themselves and is a useful strategy to use in other situations.

For children who like to get a quick result for their efforts, the 'Wizard Wand' is a great activity because it can be quickly followed by lots of running around waving the wand! For those children who can sit for longer you can extend many of these arts and crafts activities by getting out the coloured pens or letting them add glitter or glue on pictures of their favourite TV characters.

If this section proves to be a hit with your child, then turn your mind to what else he might like to make. For instance, if he enjoyed the 'Paper Plane' activity, then perhaps you could explore some basic origami (the art of folding paper) to extend his interest and skills?

Happy cutting and sticking!

Wizard Wand

P1

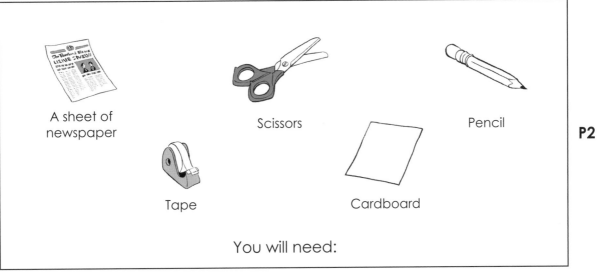

A sheet of newspaper

Scissors

Pencil

Tape

Cardboard

You will need:

P2

Get the newspaper.

P3

Fold the newspaper in half.

P4

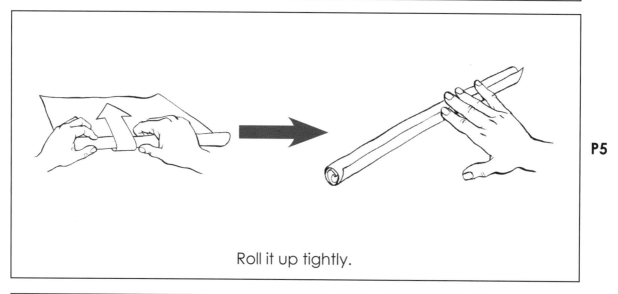

Roll it up tightly.

P5

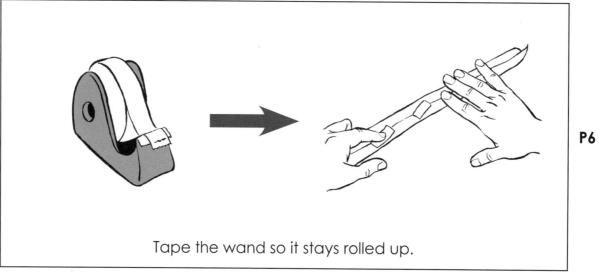

Tape the wand so it stays rolled up.

P6

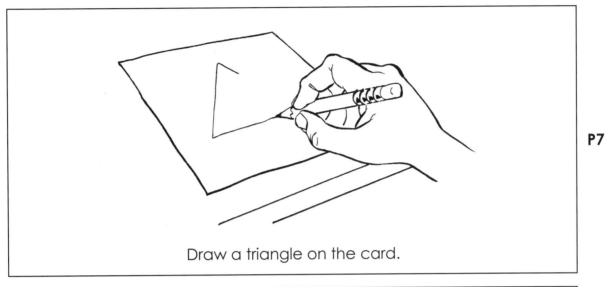

Draw a triangle on the card.

P7

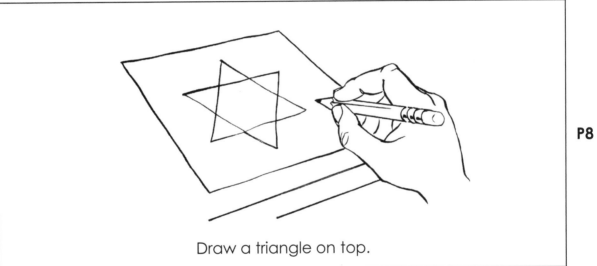

Draw a triangle on top.

P8

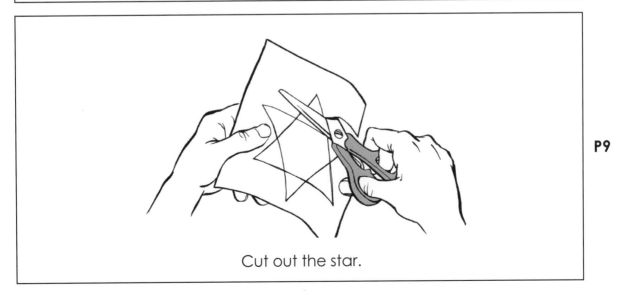

Cut out the star.

P9

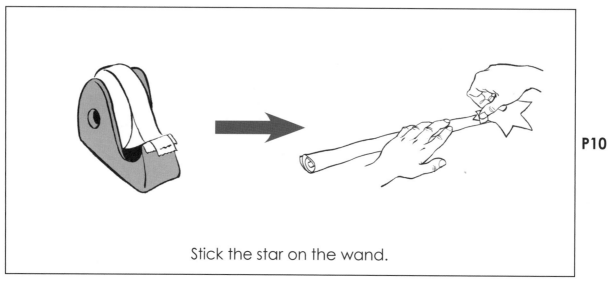

Stick the star on the wand.

P10

Pretend to be a wizard!

P11

SCRIPT 6.2 PICTURE FRAME

Picture
Frame

P1

| 4 popsicle /lolly sticks | Cardboard | A picture or photo | Colouring pens | Glue | Decorations |

P2

Get everything ready.

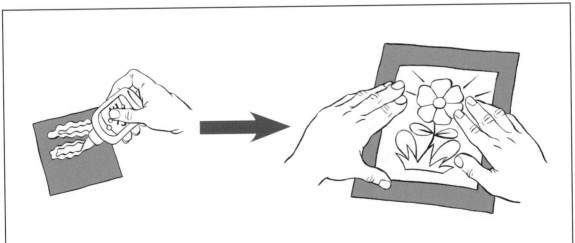

P3

Glue your picture onto the cardboard.

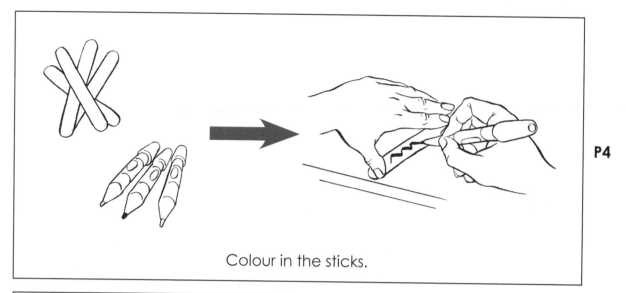

Colour in the sticks.

P4

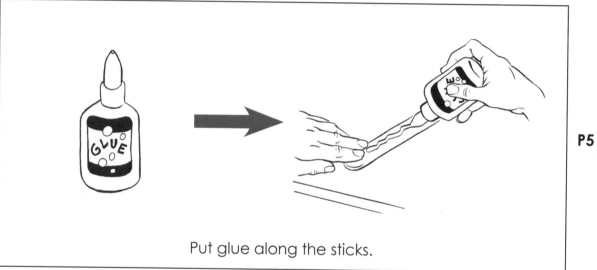

Put glue along the sticks.

P5

Put the sticks around the picture.

P6

Decorate your picture frame.

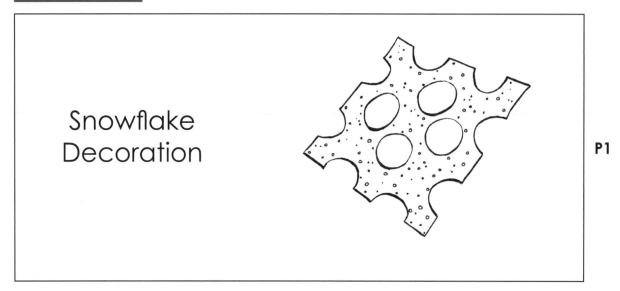

Snowflake Decoration

P1

| White paper | Pencil | Scissors | Ribbon | Glue | Glitter |

Get everything out.

P2

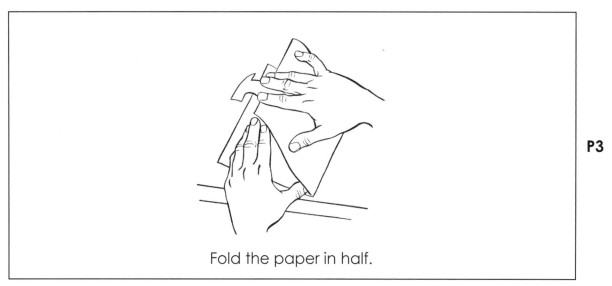

Fold the paper in half.

P3

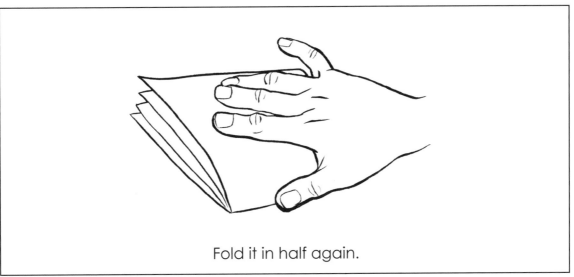

Fold it in half again.

P4

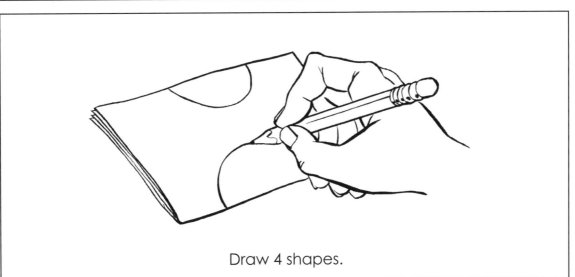

Draw 4 shapes.

P5

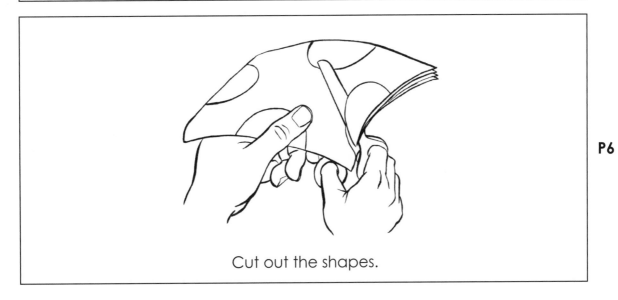

Cut out the shapes.

P6

Open the snowflake.

P7

Put some glue on the snowflake.

P8

Decorate the snowflake with glitter.

P9

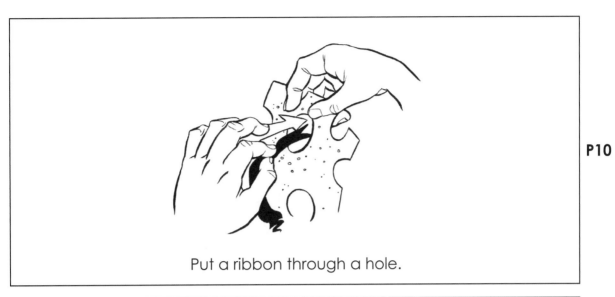

Put a ribbon through a hole.

P10

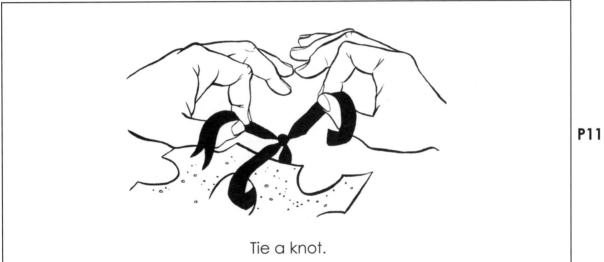

Tie a knot.

P11

Hang up your decoration.

P12

Paper
Plane

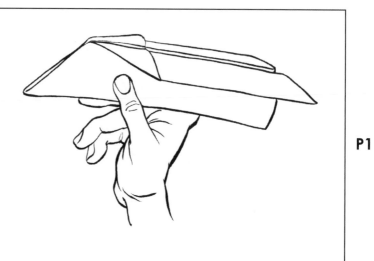

P1

Get a piece of paper.

P2

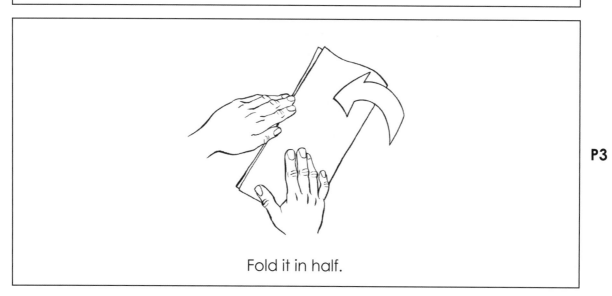

Fold it in half.

P3

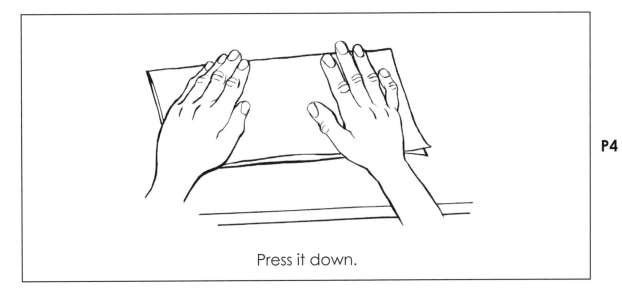

Press it down.

P4

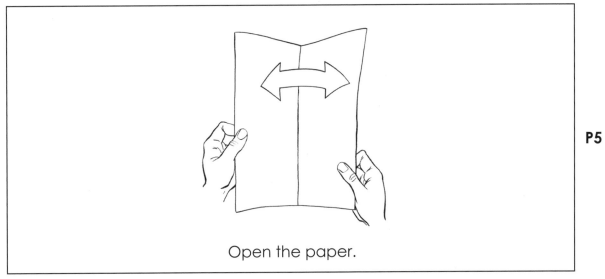

Open the paper.

P5

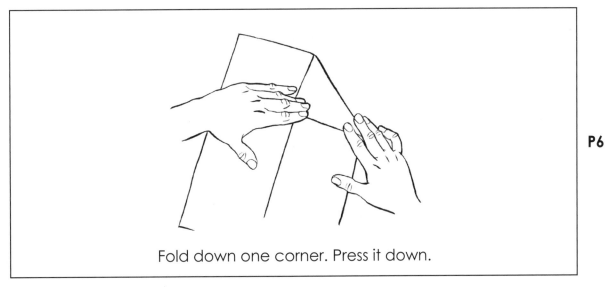

Fold down one corner. Press it down.

P6

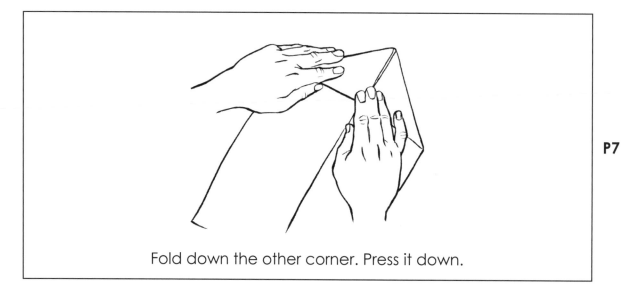

Fold down the other corner. Press it down.

P7

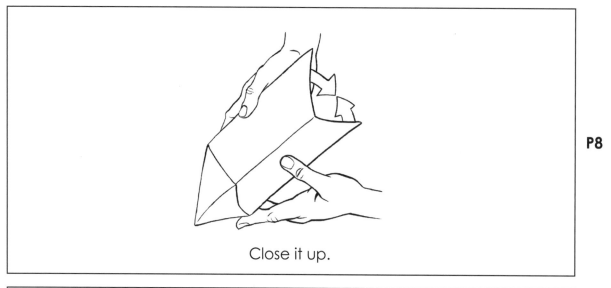

Close it up.

P8

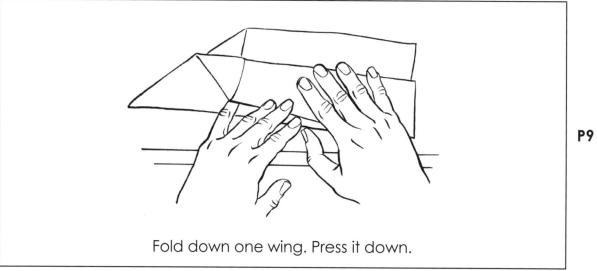

Fold down one wing. Press it down.

P9

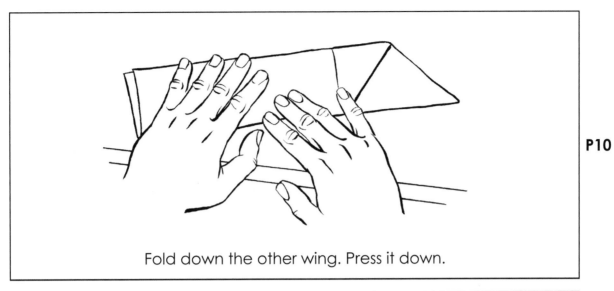

Fold down the other wing. Press it down.

P10

Throw your aeroplane and watch it fly.

P11

Balloon Person

P1

Balloon   Glue   Paper   Colouring pens

Pencil   Scissors   Cardboard

Get everything ready.

P2

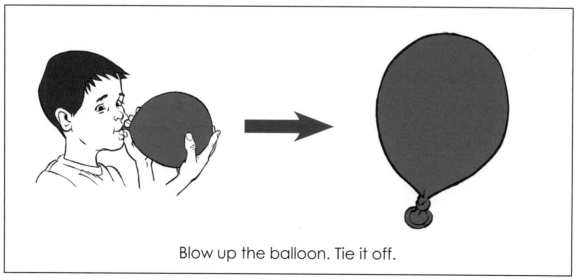

Blow up the balloon. Tie it off.

P3

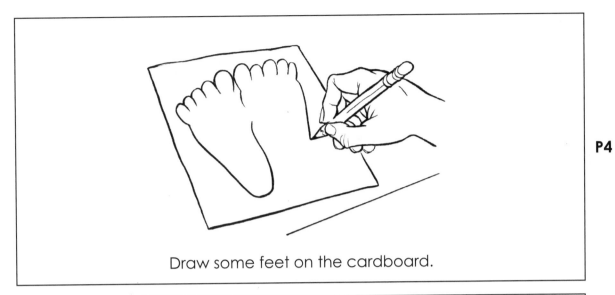

Draw some feet on the cardboard.

P4

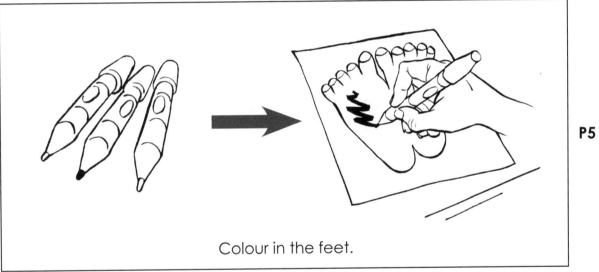

Colour in the feet.

P5

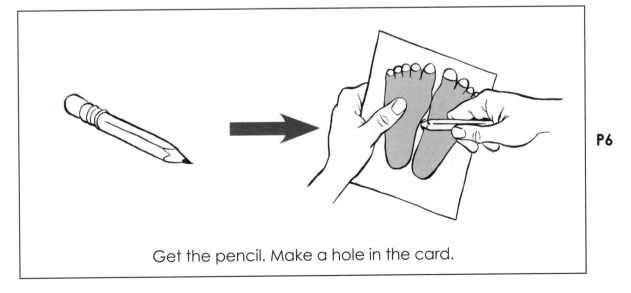

Get the pencil. Make a hole in the card.

P6

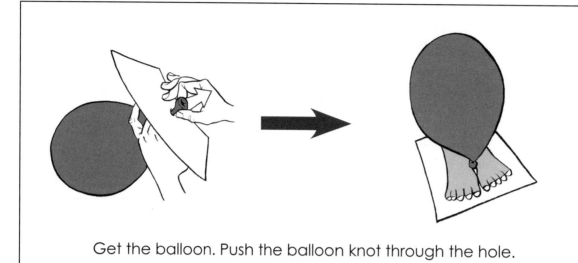

Get the balloon. Push the balloon knot through the hole.

P7

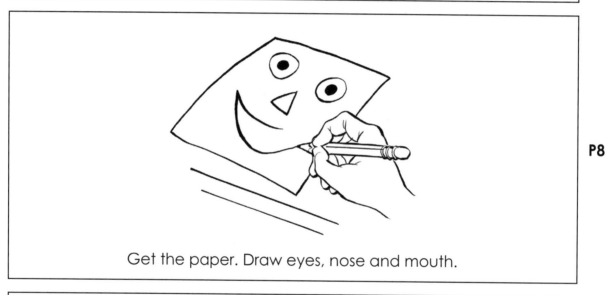

Get the paper. Draw eyes, nose and mouth.

P8

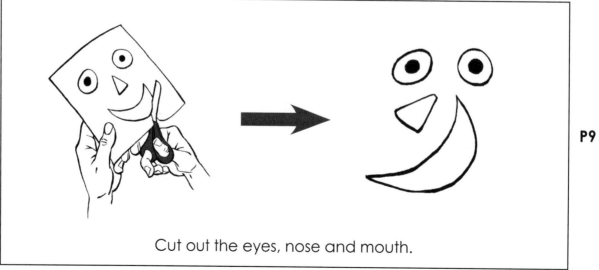

Cut out the eyes, nose and mouth.

P9

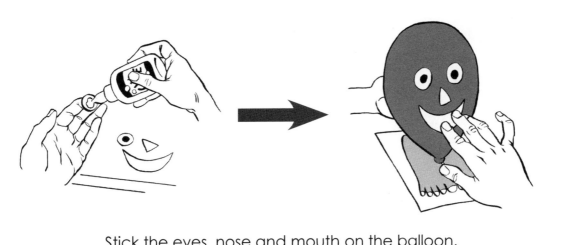

Stick the eyes, nose and mouth on the balloon.

P10

Your balloon person is ready.

P11

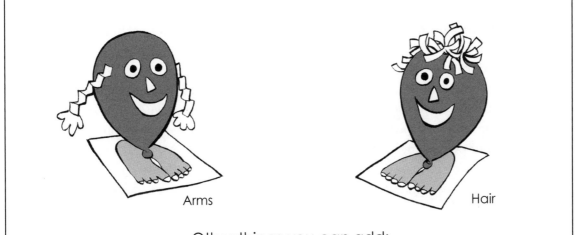

Arms

Hair

Other things you can add:

P12

Chapter 7

EVERYDAY LIVING

INTRODUCTION

Many children love to watch their parents carry out household tasks and even very young children will try to copy them sweeping the floor or stirring a pan. Children with autism often struggle to copy actions, so it can take them longer to learn basic chores and life skills. The picture scripts in this chapter provide a helping hand with this. They take children through some general household jobs step-by-step, showing them what to do. Some of the activities will also be useful in school settings where there is a focus on acquiring life skills.

Experience has taught us that it is never too soon to start helping children with autism to look after themselves. It is important to think about exactly which steps are necessary to accomplish a task completely in an appropriate way. Sometimes scripts need to be adjusted to add more steps or to eliminate an unnecessary one. Be sure to adjust your scripts so they will guide your child to successfully complete the task.

Don't be put off by how much longer it will take your child to carry out a chore. Especially in the beginning, it will take more time to teach your child how to do a task than it would take for you to do it yourself. That's OK. Just remember that your long-term goal is for your child to develop the ability to accomplish these tasks independently. Start small and allow enough time. For instance, perhaps your child could begin by washing up his plastic plate after his afternoon snack. If you want him to learn to make his bed then why not make it together, and then gradually remove your help as he becomes more accomplished, leaving just the picture script to help him?

Sensory sensitivities can make brushing teeth a tough activity for some children with autism. For some children in this situation, using the picture script makes the task more predictable and reduces their anxiety.

These picture scripts will help to teach your child skills which will serve him well through the rest of his life. We have chosen five basic daily tasks as samples where picture scripts have proven most helpful in our clinical experience. What else would you like your child to learn? Try designing your own script.

Good luck with those chores!

SCRIPT 7.1   MAKE THE BED

Make
the Bed

P1

Pull the covers up.

P2

Put the pillow on the bed.

P3

Smooth the bed out.

P4

Put pyjamas under the pillow.

P5

Put stuffed animals on the bed.

P6

Wash Your Hands

P1

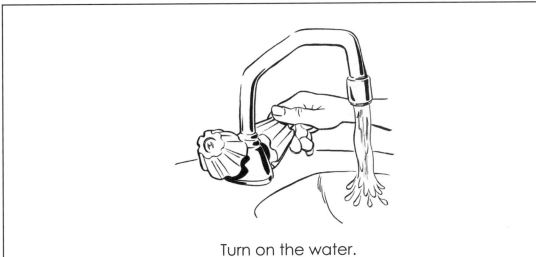

Turn on the water.

P2

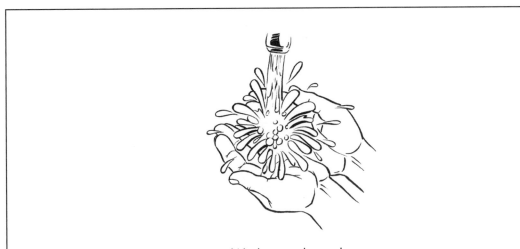

Wet your hands.

P3

Get some soap on your hands.

P4

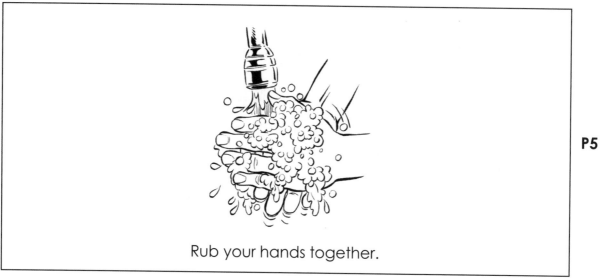

Rub your hands together.

P5

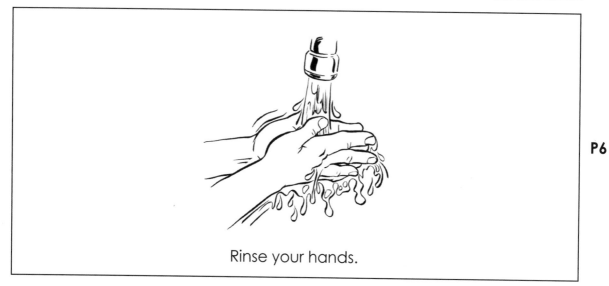

Rinse your hands.

P6

Turn off the water.

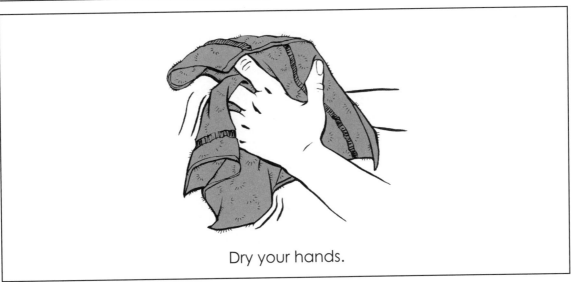

Dry your hands.

Wash the Dishes

P1

Put the dishes in the sink.

P2

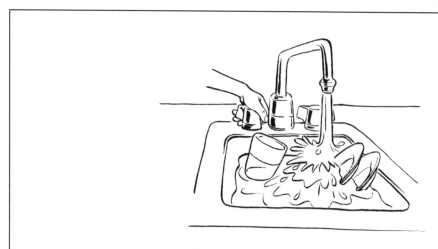

Fill the sink with warm water.

P3

Squeeze in washing detergent.

P4

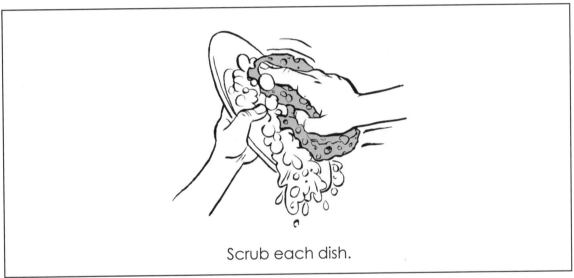

Scrub each dish.

P5

Put the clean dishes in the rack.

P6

Dry the dishes.

Put them away.

SCRIPT 7.4   SET THE TABLE

Set the Table

P1

| Placemats | Plates | Forks | Knives | Spoons | Cups |

P2

Get everything ready.

P3

Put placemats on the table.

Put plates on the placemats.

P4

Put out forks.

P5

Put out knives.

P6

Put out spoons.

P7

Put out cups.

P8

The table is ready.

P9

Brush
Your Teeth

P1

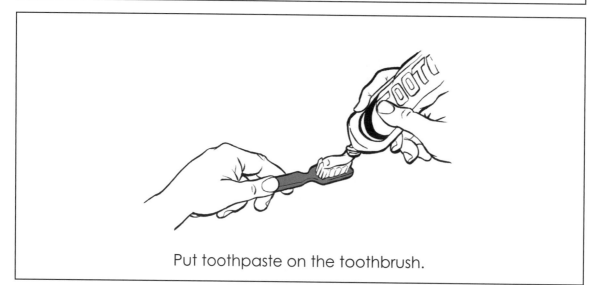

Put toothpaste on the toothbrush.

P2

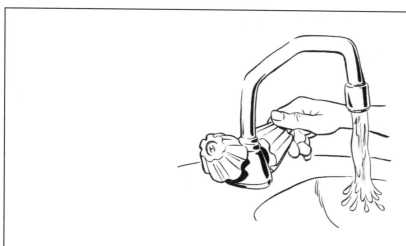

Turn on the water.

P3

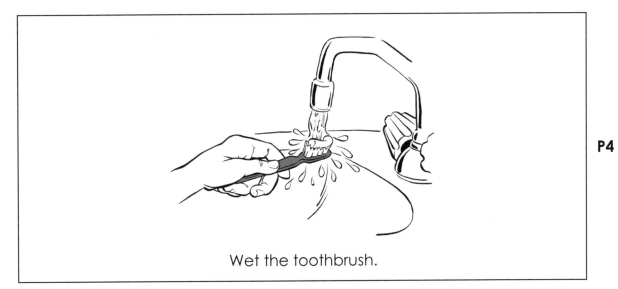

Wet the toothbrush.

P4

Brush your teeth.

P5

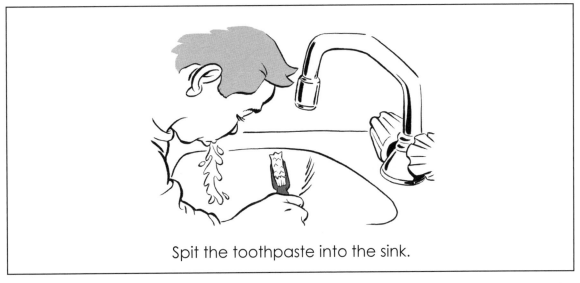

Spit the toothpaste into the sink.

P6

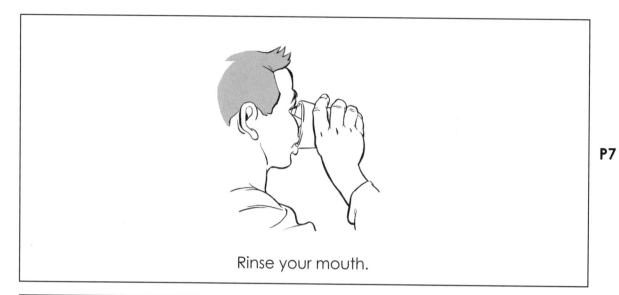

Rinse your mouth.

P7

Spit the water into the sink.

P8

Rinse your toothbrush.

P9

Turn off the water.

USEFUL RESOURCES

Here is a selection of books and websites covering some useful approaches to helping children with autism.

Caldwell, P. (2005) *Finding You Finding Me: Using Intensive Interaction to get in Touch with People Whose Severe Learning Disabilities are Combined with Autistic Spectrum Disorder.* London: Jessica Kingsley Publishers.

Frost, L.A. and Bondy, A.S. (2002) *The Picture Exchange Communication System: Training Manual* (2nd edn). Newark, DE: Pyramid Educational Products.

Grandin, T. and Panek, R. (2013) *The Autistic Brain: Thinking Across the Spectrum.* Boston, MA: Houghton Mifflin Harcourt.

Gray, C. (2010) *The New Social Story Book, Revised and Expanded 10th Anniversary Edition: Over 150 Social Stories that Teach Everyday Social Skills to Children with Autism or Asperger's Syndrome, and their Peers.* Arlington, TX: Future Horizons.

Griffin, S. and Sandler, D. (2010) *Motivate to Communicate: 300 Games and Activities for Your Child with Autism.* London: Jessica Kingsley Publishers.

Hodgdon, A.L. (1999) *Solving Behavior Problems in Autism: Improving Communication with Visual Strategies.* Troy, MI: QuirkRoberts.

Hodgdon, A.L. (2011) *Visual Strategies for Improving Communication: Practical Supports for Autism Spectrum Disorders* (revised edn). Troy, MI: QuirkRoberts.
www.AutismFamilyonline.com
www.UseVisualStrategies.com

Kranowitz, C. and Newman, J. (2010) *Growing an In-Sync Child: Simple, Fun Activities to Help Every Child Develop, Learn, and Grow.* New York, NY: Penguin Group.

Miller, L. (2006) *Sensational Kids: Hope and Help for Children with Sensory Processing Disorder (SPD).* New York, NY: Penguin Group.

Murray, S. and Noland, B. (2012) *Video Modeling for Young Children with Autism Spectrum Disorders: A Practical Guide for Parents and Professionals.* London: Jessica Kingsley Publishers.

Notbohm, E. (2012) *Ten Things Every Child with Autism Wishes You Knew* (updated and expanded edn). Arlington, TX: Future Horizons.

Rogers, S., Dawson, G. and Vismara, L. (2012) *An Early Start for Your Child with Autism: Using Everyday Activities to Help Kids Connect, Communicate, and Learn.* New York, NY: Guilford Press.

Sher, B. (2009) *Early Intervention Games: Fun, Joyful Ways to Develop Social and Motor Skills in Children with Autism Spectrum or Sensory Processing Disorders.* New York, NY: John Wiley and Sons.

Siegel, B. (2007) *Helping Children with Autism Learn: Treatment Approaches for Parents and Professionals.* New York, NY: Oxford University Press.

Stagnetti, K. (2009) *Learn to Play. A Practical Program to Develop a Child's Imaginative Play*. Melbourne, VIC: Coordinates Publisher.

Sussman, F. (1999) *More than Words: Helping Parents Promote Communication and Social Skills in Children with Autistic Spectrum Disorders*. Toronto, ON: The Hanen Centre.

Sussman, F. (2006) *TalkAbility: People Skills for Verbal Children on the Autism Spectrum – A Guide for Parents*. Toronto, ON: The Hanen Centre.

Szatmari, P. (2004) *A Mind Apart: Understanding Children with Autism and Asperger Syndrome*. New York, NY: Guilford Press.

Winner, M.G. (2008) *Think Social! A Social Thinking Curriculum for School-Age Students* (2nd edn). San Jose, CA: Think Social Publishing.

Yack, E., Aquilla, P. and Sutton, S. (2002) *Building Bridges Through Sensory Integration: Therapy for Children with Autism and Other Pervasive Developmental Disorders* (2nd edn). Las Vegas, NV: Sensory Resources.